TABLE OF CONTENTS

Unless otherwise indicated, all Scripture quotations are taken from the King James Version of the Bible.
Why Men Stay Poor
ISBN: 1-56394-578-9/B-370
Copyright © 2014 by Mike Murdock
All publishing rights belong exclusively to Wisdom International
Editor/Publisher: Deborah Murdock Johnson
Published by The Wisdom Center
4051 Denton Hwy. · Fort Worth, Texas 76117
1-817-759-BOOK · 1-817-759-2665 · 1-817-759-0300
MikeMurdockBooks.com

∽ 1 ∽

YOUR PROSPERITY IS YOUR DECISION

God Desires You To Prosper.

"Father we love hearing Your voice. When we hear Your voice we change. The best comes out of us when You talk to us. We feel a hope about life. We feel a zeal. We feel an authority, a supernatural authority over the events of our life. We are not bouncing back and reacting and responding to everything that happens, but will take initiative on our life. We believe that it is not your decision for our Prosperity. It is our decision.

"It Is God's Desire That We Prosper.

"We are designed to prosper and increase.

"The mantle of Wisdom that rests upon me was given to me by God to help people prosper.

"We believe that it's Your desire and Your design for us to prosper. I come into a Covenant with You, Lord, I come into a Covenant with You that we will see a supernatural breakthrough in our finances today. And it will not just be a Miracle. It will be a mantle of Wisdom that will come upon us and will change us and bring supernatural breakthrough.

"We receive Your anointing, not only to speak, but to hear, to understand, to listen. I pray for my extended family there at their house, their home, wherever they are in the world, in Brazil, Nigeria and England, in Nepal, all through the world, as they are a part of our family here at The Wisdom Center. I ask You today to give me swift, swift understanding of people's lives more than ever in Jesus' Name. Amen."

When the Lord stirs my heart, nothing else matters. I drop everything to obey the prompting. When I do so, there is a grace that comes upon me to fulfill my Assignment. This grace and anointing will come on you in this area, too.

The Difference In People Is The Voice They Trust.

I Cannot Change Your Life Until I Change The Voice You Honor.

I would love to tell you that if you had a really smart daddy, you would succeed. It is not true.

Absalom and Solomon had the same daddy, King David, and their outcomes were no where near the same. One of them was a fool, but Jesus referenced the other, Solomon, hundreds of years later saying he was the wisest man who ever lived.

We are studying *Why Men Stay Poor.* I have more facts and thoughts to share with you.

It is *unwise* to be poor.

It is *unnatural* to be poor.

It is *unscriptural* to be poor.

It is *unnecessary* to be poor.

It is almost stupid to stay poor after you have become acquainted with God, His laws and His ways.

You Can Only Conquer Something That You Hate. So if you are going to look for the 5 blessings of being poor, I am not your man.

I do not know any blessings of being poor.

"Dr. Mike, you do not have to pay insurance

because you do not have anything."

Well, okay. We can get really down to it. You also could never have to worry about your house being broken into because you do not have one. The homeless do not have to pay. Isn't that nice? Wouldn't that be nice to be homeless? No taxes. Does that excite you?

Of course you say, "Not really." A normal human would rather have to pay taxes and have a house than not to pay taxes.

I was raised poor. I wasn't raised starving, and I did not live in a tent, but when I wanted to go to Bible School, my father could not pay $4.00 a day to put me through Southwestern Assemblies of God Bible College. We were only talking about $4.00 per cotton-pickin' day.

I did not think much about it then because I hadn't studied, and did not really know much. I was taught you make what you have go around. That is the philosophy we are dealing with here.

Your Philosophy Decides If You Stay Poor. Your philosophy of life, how you look at life, determines your income.

I well remember the young man at school who had a big lunch box. It was really nice. I had the big paper sacks Daddy got from Weingarten's.

Let me explain my paper sack meals from my background. Mother kept all of her big paper bags. My mother would put the little sandwiches in the bottom of the bag. Yes, there were butter sandwiches sometimes made with just butter.

I never had two pieces of bologna on the same sandwich and I did not like to fold over a piece of bread because then I felt like I would only had a half a sandwich. That would mess my head up.

Anyway, Daddy could not put me through school at Southwestern Assemblies of God Bible College. The cost was $550.00 a semester, about $4.00 a day.

I made a record of my piano playing and I sold it over at the Girls' Dormitory for $1.00. In those days it was very good to be single at 18, because all the single girls would buy your record thinking that was part of the investment in a friendship. I would usually come back to my dorm with $10.00 or $15.00 in sales.

Eventually, I got a job in Dallas. A friend of mine, Wayne McKenzie, was son of the CEO of the largest Sears store in the world. He was a Christian man. We were all friends, and I stayed in their home on occasion. Through that relationship with Wayne I was able to get a job and make some money.

It doesn't feel good to have no money. I get amused at people who say, "Money won't make you happy." Well, your leg won't either, so why do not we just cut it off. Your ear won't make you happy, so let's cut it off.

Usually I laugh and respond, "You say money won't make you happy, but how would you know since you have never had any?"

The Bible says in Ecclesiastes 10:19, "Money answereth all things." Nobody quite believes that. No preacher will preach that, of course, because it creates too many questions, but the fact is almost everything you want in life comes through money.

The Purpose of Money Is To Create Experiences, Feelings.

Human beings are obsessed with feelings.

There is not a father in the world that does not want to provide an environment of protection for his family. There is no dad in the world that doesn't want to buy something for his baby, and every mother wants to dress up her little baby with the cutest clothes.

Everybody wants to have options. "Would you like something to drink? We have water in a small glass, and we have water in a tin glass. Would you like some other options? Would you like a Coke? Would you like iced tea?"

Through the Catholic Church and the centuries of time, people begin to sell poor people the idea that poverty was partially spiritual. Out of that thinking arose our heroes like Mother Teresa and Mahatma Gandhi. Both of whom learned you can't do anything without money.

There is nothing like poor people sticking together against people who have money. Politicians began to use poverty to win votes. The interests of the rich were pitted against the poor. From there began the hatred and class warfare.

The thinking became, "You've got money? I do not. Scripturally, you should be giving me your money." Have you ever heard that kind of story?

The fact is that every one of us is of the offspring of The Most High God and He has invested in every single one of us. He has invested ideas, energy, thoughts and relationships.

He has placed the potential for Favor in every one of us, and none of us have thoroughly investigated the Divine investments in us.

I am the thoughts of God. I am what God came up with. The entire universe that was created by Him. I am His offspring. You are His offspring.

I want you to develop a hatred of poverty. The best thing you can do for the poor is not be one of them. The best thing you can do for somebody drowning is not drown with them so you can pick them up.

The Bible Is A Book About Prosperity.

There are two paths; the paths of rebellion; the paths of obedience. I believe when I lose money, I have broken a law of God.

There are 72 laws I look at. One is the Law of Adaptation. Did I fail to adapt? Did I fail to adapt to expectations?

I study how to prosper. It does not take much money to survive. There is only so much food you can eat. You can feed yourself by visiting the feeding programs of churches in The United States.

We have a collection of people that are just like me. They feel good when they bless somebody. There are enough people in Fort Worth who think this way, that people do not have to work a lick to get food.

In fact, there are people who will feed you if you knock on their door and say, "I am hungry." You can ask for a loaf of bread, and they will invite you in, give you what you need for two meals and invite you to stay for supper. If you act real sleepy and you look like you are very tired, and ask about a place to get some sleep, they will give you a place to sleep, too.

So if your goal is to take care of you, there is not much to it. But there is a lot more to prospering and thriving.

The More Important People Become To You The More Valuable Prosperity Becomes To You.

The more important helping somebody becomes to you, the more you will desire to prosper.

When Bishop Saúl González walked me through the dump in Puerto Vallarta, I saw kids everywhere.

They were running their fingers inside trying to get some kind of food.

Bishop González told me, "There are 1,000 kids here." He began to cry and asked, "Dr. Murdock, will you help me feed these children?"

Linda Knight, a lady minister, a pastor's wife from Seattle, Washington, that I preached for often, was there just hours before she was killed in an airplane crash. Linda said, "You're my mentor. I have my ministry because of you. Would you help me feed these kids?"

Bishop González told me, "Mike, these kids are digging through the trash trying to find a banana peel, or an apple core to see if there is anything left of the apple."

Bishop González told me through tears, "I have a staff, but we do not have money."

I said, "Until Jesus returns or I die, I will feed every one of these children." I made a decision that day.

Has it taken tens of thousands and tens of thousands of dollars? You bet your life it has, but I have a Jehovah-jireh in my life. I am the son of The King of the Universe.

He is the King of kings, and He said anything I would ask in His Name is something He will do. He said, "Because you do what I say, you can ask anything that you will."

There is a criterion for anything you want to receive from God. *There are requirements.*

There are *qualifying* swims in the Olympics.

There is a *qualification* run for the Olympics.

There are *qualifications* for financial blessing.

There are *qualification* drives for all the car races

in Daytona.

If I go to a doctor because I have a toothache, I do not want him to say, "Your ear is working well. Why do not we just be thankful for your ear?"

"My tooth is killing me."

"Look at your legs, they feel good. Let's just be thankful for your legs."

No, I want to get my tooth taken care of. I am not going to tell you, "Praise God. At least you can breathe. Praise God, you are not in the hospital today. Hallelujah."

Those are worthy things, but I want to address financial poverty. I am addressing *Why Men Stay Poor.*

It is Not God's Fault And It is Not God's Plan For A Man To Have Nothing.

Deuteronomy Chapter 28. Read this for yourself. I hate the anti-Prosperity spirit because it's like stripping warriors of their guns, swords, and spears because a weaponless warrior has no impact. There is nothing to fear from someone who has no weapon.

The Bible has an interesting illustration where there was a man in a city who knew a strategy. The Bible tells us he was a wise man, but because he had no money, nobody trusted his counsel. Because he had no money, nobody believed his advice.

Financial Prosperity Multiplies Influence. People will listen to prosperous men 1,000 times sooner than they will listen to someone who has no money.

If I said, "We have a real genius at The Wisdom Center. He will teach you how to lose 20 pounds in 20 days." I would come hear that guy.

But if I saw him and he weighed 350 pounds I probably would not believe him when he said, "I am here to teach you how to lose 20 pounds in 20 days."

I would probably say, "I am going to wait until I see him get a little skinnier."

I told one of my friends who was real heavy, "Don't be talking about fasting. It makes you look like a hypocrite."

"Why do not you preach on fasting Mike?" I would look like a hypocrite, because I have not been fasting.

When We Prosper Our Voice Is Amplified, Our Influence Is Amplified.

I do prosper. I am not a poor preacher. I am not starving. I am not begging. I am not pleading. And I am not hoping I make my house note next month. I am not going from paycheck to paycheck and it's amazing.

I went in to buy some gold yesterday, and there was no response. They threw all the business to a young girl there, because they did not know I had any money.

I was wearing my jogging outfit, and some tennis shoes, but it wasn't 10 minutes until I brought out a little money to buy the gold and even the security guard was advising me on gold.

They all gathered around. I do not think anybody was sitting there.

I said, "I do not know anything about gold, but I want to know. Start teaching me and telling me what I need to know. Why is this gold more important than this gold?" They started to explain when I demonstrated my qualifications.

They told me some of the gold coins I was looking at came from companies, while some others came from the government.

I said, "I want some $50.00 gold pieces."

They did not have any $50.00 gold pieces. When you travel, you have to report anything over $10,000.00 to customs, but you can carry a $50.00 gold piece, and you only have to report the $50.00.

So it may be worth, you know, $10,000.00, but you do not have to report it. So there are just various things that you learn as you go along. But it was so funny, because they all became very responsive when they found out I had some money.

It was just like when your child gets very excited when they see daddy has a little money. They experience all kinds of toy concepts then.

Deuteronomy 28 talks about *The Blessing of The Lord*.

One preacher friend said, "I found a way for the Prosperity message to be accepted. It is to talk about *The Spirit of Generosity*." He said, "Everybody accepts that phrase, *The Spirit of Generosity*."

I have another preacher friend, he calls it *The Blessed Life*. It appears spiritual, non-greedy, holy; *The Blessed Life*.

Everybody says, "Oh, good. It is not Prosperity, just the blessed life." You can call it any cotton-pickin' thing you need that motivates and inspires you. I do not Mind any of it, but Prosperity is a gift from the Lord. It is a blessing from the Lord.

It is a good thing.

It is a good thing.

It is a good thing.

I want to give you some reasons Why Men Stay Poor. The first reason is very Scriptural.

1. An Unteachable Spirit. The reason men stay poor is they can't learn from anybody prosperous.

It doesn't matter what country it is, they want America to underwrite them. They say, "Give us $2,000,000,000.00 to help our people." Others may say, "Give us $5,000,000,000.00 and we will let you put your Navy here to help you feel more safe." There is a trade out, but the fact is poor nations resent those nations with money.

I have said this about 17,000 times, *You Cannot Learn From Someone You Resent.*

2. You Cannot Learn From Someone You Resent. Now you understand why Donald Trump gave his son $5.00 a week as an allowance. He said, "They have to learn the value of money and what it takes to get it." Wealthy people are very sensitive about their children learning. This is why some do not leave their children anything.

Deuteronomy 28, "It shall come to pass if…"

Circle the word "if" in your Bible. God was saying, "I want to qualify you for the blessing I am about to discuss with you. I want to talk to you about this blessed life. If thou shalt hearken diligently unto the voice of The Lord thy God to observe and to do all…" Circle "all." If you leave one ingredient out, you change the outcome.

The chemical name for water is H_2O. The chemical combination is two parts hydrogen, and one part oxygen. Two parts of hydrogen is good, so surely two parts oxygen would be good. Let's have H_2O_2. Then you have hydrogen peroxide which, if misused, can kill you. If you tamper with Divine equations you create a deadly consequence, and the Bible is about rewards and consequences.

Deuteronomy 28:1, "If thou shalt hearken

diligently unto the voice of the Lord thy God, to observe and to do all His Commandments…" I can't drop $10.00 in the Offering, turn around and slap my wife, and think my Offering will qualify me for *Divine* Favor. I just messed my wife up. The Bible says if you even get in an argument with your wife, God stops listening to you. Some readers may think, "That means He has hardly ever heard me."

He says to make things right with your wife before you attempt to get along with authority. God said, "If you can't get along with your wife, then you have got a problem with Me." Let's work on getting along with the wife.

Let's continue reading Deuteronomy 28:1, "…to observe and to do all His commandments which I command thee this day…" Then He describes the rewards of Divine instructions obeyed. "…that the Lord thy God will set thee on high above all nations of the earth."

He is talking about *promotion, influence* and *Prosperity.* We often say, "The man with the gold makes the rules."

If I pay the bills, I make the rules.

If I pay for the house, I make the rules.

If I buy the house, I decide the color it is.

If I buy the furniture, I decide where it sits.

If I buy the car, I decide how fast I drive…*unless I want to pay a fine.*

The whole point is when you obey God, He starts talking about how this is what will happen to you. He starts talking about places of influence, places of power, places of achievement and promotion. He says, "Listening to Me will produce this for you. Honoring

Me will produce this result for you."

I believe in *Prosperity*.

I believe in *owning more than one house*.

I believe in *having a house big enough*.

I believe in *having a house paid for*.

I believe in *your car being paid for*.

I believe in having such a life in God that He is our Jehovah-jireh. He provides for us. He blesses us, and He promotes us. *I believe the secret is in honoring the instructions of God in His Word.*

He requires honesty. He said, "Let your words be yay, or nay."

I have had to deal with a lot of lying in my environment. You cannot tolerate lying in your presence, even by a talented person you enjoy. I stopped one young man a few weeks ago and said, "Son, you have so many pluses to you, but you lie. Does your wife know you lie? Do your kids know you lie?"

He hung his head and said, "No."

I said, "I hope they do not ever find out you are a liar." I was trying to train him for the ministry. I said, "Son, I do not care how good you look, or how much you love to praise God, you have to start telling the truth."

There is reward in telling the truth. I remember watching the presidential debates. It was a challenge to keep my mouth shut.

I made some mistakes. I tweeted something and The Holy Spirit dealt with me so strongly I had to tweet my apologies. What I said was disrespectful, and I had no business saying it. Many of us find keeping our mouth shut is the greatest challenge of life.

I hate lying. Everybody has their things they strongly dislike. Some people hate cocaine. I do not love cocaine, I have never used it. Some people hate drinking. I have never drank in my life, but I do not have a hatred for drinking, but lying messes my head up.

I can't make good decisions when somebody lies to me. All my decisions will be wrong if the data is not right because *you lied to me.*

The young man said, "I did not lie about everything, just one thing."

"Give me a map," I said. "You tell me to turn left when it should have been right and I wind up in the wrong country."

3. Men Stay Poor Because They Do Not Trust The Character of God. God is saying, "Follow My counsel. You can trust Me."

There is only one reason a man sins, he doesn't believe in a consequence. He doesn't believe The Word of God.

Every time we sin we're saying, "I really do not believe in this consequence. I do not believe anything will happen to me. I believe I can lie and nothing will happen. I believe I can cheat on my income tax, and nothing will happen. I believe I can lie to my wife and nothing will happen."

God is saying here, "I want you to be very aware of a reward system and a consequence system." I do not linger much on the consequence, because I tend to teach to the obedient. I do not really talk much to the rebellious. I want the rebellious to taste their consequences.

I am really for the obedient. I am called to the obedient. Let's keep reading in Deuteronomy 28, "The Lord thy God will set thee on high above all nations of the earth." God is appealing here to an innate need to have authority. It is in us. We were created with a Divine sense of authority.

I was made to rule. You were made to reign... R-E-I-G-N. You were made to rule on the earth. God said to Adam, "I am going to give you a garden." God is *constantly* looking for Receivers. God has so much stuff, and His stuff is being multiplied. It is being multiplied exponentially, and continuously.

Everything God created multiplies. Imagine the excitement of a scientist saying, "We have found 29 more planets. They are probably older than earth." Every time man finds something he is so ecstatic.

We could live 10,000 lives and not see it all, because everything God creates keeps creating. Do you understand that? God doesn't just create something and say, "There it is."

God is a God of multiplication. Remember the first instruction He gave to Adam. (See Genesis 1:28.) Multiply. Replenish.

God Expects Everything To Increase. God hates anything that doesn't grow. He looked at the man with one talent, and took it away. Obviously God looks at things in the opposite way of what our government does.

God said, "This man was given one talent and did not do anything with it."

He did not say, "This guy doesn't have enough, so I am going to take a couple of talents from the guy that has 5 talents."

Jesus did not "feel sorry" for the man with one talent. No, Jesus was so upset with the lack of productivity He stripped the guy who would not use his one talent and gave it to the guy who had 5. (Read Matthew 25:29-31.)

4.   Men Stay Poor When They Envy The Prosperous.

5.   Men Stay Poor Because They Do Not Learn From Producers. The *Bible* puts it this way, "Poverty and shame will come to him that refuseth instruction," (Proverbs 13:18). If I am in poverty the Bible says there is an instruction I have refused to follow. From who? God, or a man.

The Bible says in Deuteronomy 5:16, if I Honor my mother and father it will go well with me all the days of my life. God will give you what you need.

"Well, Dr. Mike, why should I get excited over God when the government will do that?"

Deuteronomy 28:2, "All these blessings shall come on thee, and overtake thee…" Does it say blessings will overtake you because God loves you?

No. Prosperity has nothing to do with Divine love. Divine Prosperity is completely unrelated to Divine love. There are people I love, but they do not get any money from me. I love them, but they do not inspire my giving.

If you ever find any person in your life that makes you want to give to them, *celebrate them.* They will keep you blessed all your life. There are plenty of people around you that do not want to give them anything. You do not know why.

There is a girl I really liked one time. She was good looking. She had it all, but I had no desire to give to her.

There are 12 proofs of love, and one of the proofs of love is a desire to listen. One of the proofs of love is a passion to protect, a passion to pleasure somebody.

But the greatest proof of love is explained in John 3:16, "For God so loved the world, that He gave..." *The Greatest Proof of Love Is When You Want To Give To Somebody.* That is the proof of love.

That is the proof of love. And I did not want to give her anything. I did not want to buy her clothes. I did not want to buy her a car. And sure enough, I thought, "Well this is crazy, I just know I like her, I just know."

But I looked at that. I had no desire to give. There were reasons for that. But He says that giving is a reaction of love.

Here's what He says in Deuteronomy 28:1, "If thou shalt hearken diligently unto the voice of The Lord thy God..." God talks more than anybody you have met.

If you have been exposed to my ministry at all, you know that the most powerful thing in the universe is conversation. *God rules His whole world through conversation.*

6. Men Stay Poor Because of What They Say. What you say about your life really matters. If you begin to give excuses for your poverty you will stay poor. Some stay in the trap of poverty by saying, "I dropped out of high school. I never went to college."

We have people that never finished high school who are billionaires. So you can't say that the reason you are broke is because you have no education. Some of the stupidest people in the world have Ph.D.'s. They cannot fit in with other people. There are people with degrees who are laying around in the ghettos.

Deuteronomy 28 is as much Bible as, "For God so loved the world..." Deuteronomy 28 is as much as, "In the beginning God created the Heavens..." This is the Bible. Verse 1, "If thou shalt hearken diligently to the voice of the Lord thy God..." Verse 3, "Blessed shalt thou be in the city, blessed shalt thou be in the field." He is trying to show you that blessing is not an event. Blessing is a world that you enter. It is a lifestyle.

Deuteronomy 28:4, "Blessed shall be the fruit of thy body, the fruit of thy ground, the fruit of thy cattle." What is He saying here? Anything connected to you will prosper. Anybody who likes you will prosper. Anybody who enjoys you will prosper. Hallelujah.

Let me stop here. Is there an advantage in *knowing* you? Is there an advantage in *liking* you? Is there any *reward* to relationship with you? There are people you know that *nothing* has happened for them since you have known them. No blessing increases. Nothing's multiplied.

There are other people that their presence alone *inspires* you, and *energizes* you. Years ago I dated a girl named Debbie. I was 36, and she worked for my music company.

She came to spend two weeks in the area, and every morning she motivated me to run. She's the one that got me running 5 miles a day. I did not want to run at all, but something about the way she talked to me motivated me toward fitness.

She would run backwards in front of me. She would say, "You can do it, you can do it." And I do not know what excited me. It may have been her legs, because she wore shorts. It may have been the way she talked to me. Something about the way she talked to me made me want to get in shape. She made me want to get right for her. After two weeks she turned around and married a friend of mine. He could play a trumpet. Maybe that was what she was looking for.

But when she ran backwards, she had a way of looking at me while saying, "You can do this thing. It is helping. It is coming off."

When she talked to me, I got excited, and eventually I would get up at 5 and run in the morning. I would run at night in the hills of Las Colinas. She excited me about my health. She energized me.

Energy is an *investment*. There are people in your life that *excite* you about life.

There are other people that make you feel like life is a longer trip than what you really wanted to take, but God wants to *improve* the journey. He encourages you by saying, "Everybody and everything around you is blessed by your presence. Even the cows that hang around you are blessed."

God has given us a picture here. He is saying, "Everything in your world becomes reproductive." There is passion in your world. There is love in your world. There is energy in your world.

He said, "If you obey Me, you become so stirred that you think you can do anything because you can."

An incredible truth is revealed in Genesis 11:6 in the story of The Tower of Babel. These were evil people worshiping demon spirits, but God said *nothing* was *impossible* for them because they *believed* nothing was impossible.

Andrew Carnegie, the wealthiest man on earth many years ago, made his fortune in steel. Mr. Carnegie met a young man named Napoleon Hill who wanted to learn the secrets of wealth and Prosperity.

Mr. Carnegie said, "Son, I am not giving you any

money. I am giving you 100 letters of introduction."

Access is your greatest gift. If somebody gives you access to their Mind, their brain, their secrets, their Wisdom, their counsel, they have given you their very best.

Access Is An Opportunity For You To Document Your Difference From Everybody Else.

I do not want you to live poor, and I want you to have the blessing of the Lord where you can ask anything that you will and it shall be done. I want you to have a voice on the earth. I want you to feel good about your family, feel good about your house, feel good about being debt-free, and there is a path to it. *There is a path to everywhere in the world.* You have to find the path.

Napoleon Hill took the 100 letters. He began to go around the world meeting these men, and when he finished meeting them face-to-face, he put all their secrets together in a book called *Think And Grow Rich.*

Throughout the astounding book were the laws of God. One was the Law of Imagination. *What you can picture you can achieve.*

These men all over the world at different levels of wealth had tapped into a Divine law. It is the power of the Mind to picture.

God talks in pictures. In Genesis 15:5 God said to Abraham, "See the stars? That is what your children will be like, Abraham. Do you see the sand of the sea? That is what your children will be like one day."

Let's go further. There is something amazing I want you to see. Deuteronomy 28:6-8, "Blessed shalt thou be when thou comest in, and blessed shalt thou be when thou goest out. The Lord shall cause thine enemies that rise up against thee to be smitten before thy face: they shalt come out against thee one way, and flee before thee seven ways. The Lord shall command the blessing…" Let that phrase go deep into you, "The Lord shall command the blessing."

"The Lord shall command the blessing upon thee in thy storehouses…" Pay attention to the term "storehouses." That means extra; enough for other people.

I reached enough for me a long time ago. Then God began to give me enough for other people. Hallelujah!

When He said it's more blessed to give, He means that the joy of giving *exceeds* the joy of receiving, and it actually does. You know that getting all the Christmas gifts does not compare to watching others open their gifts you bought them.

What I love about Prosperity is getting to create such ecstasy for others. You get to create such joy for others.

Deuteronomy 28:8-11, "In all that thou settest thine hand unto; and He shall bless thee in the land which the Lord thy God giveth thee. The Lord shall establish thee an holy people…And all people of the earth shall see that thou art called by the name of The Lord; and they shall be afraid of thee. And The Lord shall make thee plenteous in goods."

Is this a bad Scripture? Is this an unnecessary Scripture? Should this chapter be deleted from the Bible?

"Now, Brother Mike, I think there is a problem with greed."

God cured greed when He inserted returning the

Tithe into the equation. God knew that if He could get us returning 10 percent, it would cure the possibility of greed. Hallelujah!

The whole purpose of the Tithe is not to pay for God's food. God has never said, "Man, you did not pay your Tithe last week and I have been fasting for 3 days."

God doesn't need my Tithe so He can feed angels or finish paving the streets He started building. He doesn't need my Tithes so He can put carpet in the mansions.

The Tithe Is Proof of Honor. He says something really powerful in 28:11, "And The Lord shall make thee plenteous in goods, in the fruit of thy body, and in the fruit of thy cattle, and in the fruit of thy ground."

Verses 12-13 gets even better, "The Lord shall open unto thee His good treasure, the Heaven to give the rain unto thy land in His season, and to bless all the work of thine hand: and thou shalt lend unto many nations, and thou shalt not borrow. And the Lord shall make thee the head, and not the tail; and thou shalt be above only, and thou shalt not be beneath; if that thou hearken to the commandments of the Lord thy God, which I command thee this day, to observe and to do them."

Continue reading verse 14, "And thou shalt not go aside from any of the words which I command thee this day, to the right hand, or to the left, to go after other gods to serve them." Then He talks about what happens if you do not hearken...*Poverty.*

7. Men Stay Poor Because They Refuse To Embrace The Character of God And The Instruction To Multiply.

8. Men Stay Poor Because They Excuse

Themselves As Being Uneducated.

9.   Men Stay Poor Because They Look For Reasons To Talk Like A Victim...To Be A Victim.

10.   Men Stay Poor Because They Have No Dreams Bigger Than Their Present. You have to have a dream. You have to have a goal. Ninety-seven out of 100 Americans have never *written* down a list of their goals.

A young lady tweeted me from Nigeria, "Your books have changed my life."

I tweeted her back how much I appreciated her good words.

She tweeted me, "Is this really *the* Mike Murdock, or is this a fake tweet?"

I tweeted her back, "It is me."

She wrote back, "I have to tell you something. I planted a $58.00 Seed. I had nothing, but God gave me an idea for the government to use. The government decided they would fund my project. I went from a $58.00 Seed-sower to being a millionaire today."

Who have you decided to *trust?* What voice *matters?* Do you have a Future? What kind of Future? What do you want to *change?*

11. Men Stay Poor Because of Wrong Decisions. Men make wrong decisions about their relationships.

12. Men Stay Poor Because They Invest In Bad Soil. They do not do tests and research.

Look at the company that is losing millions and millions of dollars. Think of this cruise ship that went wrong, possibly because of a drunk captain. Think of this cruise ship. It was reported it cost $600,000,000.00. I do not know how much it cost.

Maybe more. Think of the lawsuits because of one wrong man.

One Wrong Voice Is Deadly. Some years ago, I sat down with one of my bankers. I knew nothing about mutual funds. Nothing. He said, "You need mutual funds." He named 3. "They are the best ones."

I did not know anything about mutual funds.

Warren Buffett, whose estimated worth is $49,000,000,000.00, is the number one investor in the world. One of his 5 rules is, "Don't invest in anything you do not want to know a lot about."

I lost $30,000.00 in oil. I did not want to learn about oil, I just wanted some money. I liked the people who talked to me. They were salesmen. They knew how to talk to me, how to persuade me.

On two mutual funds alone, I lost $250,000.00 in 12 months. That may not be much to some of you rich people, but a quarter of a million in 12 months? Losing $10,000.00 a year over 25 years would be bad enough. Imagine losing $250,000.00 in the first year.

Do you think I ever went back to him again for more advice? I did go back to him and say, "Do you know how much you cost me? I did what you said."

The banker said, "It'll come back around."

I said, "I do not have 100 years left of my life. I can't wait for this thing to come back around."

Who is advising you on your investments? Don't give a man $25,000.00 to invest for you until you see what he does with $5,000.00. Don't give him $5,000.00 until you have found 5 friends who made some money because of their investment.

13. Men Stay Poor Because They Really Do Not Want To Be Wealthy. If I went to your house I might see a $35,000.00 car outside your $185,000.00 home. If I wanted to see your books on wealth and you have 10, you have spent a total of $125.00. Can I believe that you want to be wealthy? *No.*

Some people want to *look* wealthy. Some of the *best* dressed people in the world are the *poorest.* They do not want to *be* wealthy, they want to *look* wealthy. I am not going to spend $2,000.00 on a suit when I can buy one for $300.00 and invest the $1,700.00 in gold.

I have a craving for people to be blessed. It started when I saw my little father, full of The Holy Ghost, praying. He loved God, but he did not have enough money to buy two slices of bologna to put on the sandwich.

I got upset. "What do you mean you can't afford $4.00 a day to put me in Bible School when you pray 4 hours a day? What kind of God do you have Dad? I do not want to be broke God."

I am in the process of changing banks. For two or 3 days in a row, I was unable to cash a little check I had. I said, "This feels a little odd when I have got more money than you. I can cash this check. I can cash it myself."

Our banks are just like this. They do not know when the money is going to go wrong. They do not know if they're going to get, it's crazy. This economy is crazy.

What do I do in this kind of economy?

You have a Jehovah-jireh who's not crazy.

He is *stable.*

He is *established,* and He loves *blessing* the obedient.

He is *looking* for somebody to bless.

He said to Adam, "I want you to receive a garden

from Me. I want you to receive a wife from Me."

He has always been a Giver. "He [Jesus] came unto His own, and His own received Him not. But as many as received Him, to them gave He power to become the sons of God," (John 1:11-12).

I fly everywhere talking about the character of God. He *wants* to bless you. He is not trying to starve you. He is not trying to see how rough He can make it for you.

He said, "See if I won't open the windows of Heaven and bless you so much that you will need to build three closets to hold your clothes," (read Malachi 3:10).

"Brother Mike, money's not important to me."

You need to listen to this so you can be good to the people paying all your bills. If you are a parasite, and somebody's paying all your bills, you need to be a thankful parasite. There is nothing as memorable as a parasite who buys you presents.

I receive *His love.*

I receive *His character.*

I receive *His instructions.*

I receive *every part of God.*

14. Men Stay Poor Because They Have Never Inventoried Divine Investments In Themselves. They are blind to the gold God has put inside of them.

15. Men Stay Poor Because They Do Not Know Who To Please.

I will give you an example: One of my relatives, a precious young man I love, worked for me. I said, "Son, I need to get about 200 cassettes made in the next 7 days or so. I feel a stirring in me."

I am a spirit man, and when the Spirit of God stirs me, *I move fast.* I remember a real estate transaction where He gave me an instruction, and in one day, 24 hours, I had a profit of $4,000,000.00.

When God talks to me, I move.

I have learned to put great value on the voice of God. He talks more than anybody you have met.

My nephew said, "Uncle Mike, we can't get these done that fast. These companies have other customers, too. They have other people they have to deal with. They have other customers."

I said, "Son, this is the Lord. I feel like we need to make these."

He did not want to do it. He did not want to call.

He started arguing with me about what I wanted. I still have some of his blood in this environment. It tries to argue me out of what I ask for.

I said, "Son, I had no idea you were working for that company. I have been paying you a salary every two weeks, and you are fighting for them instead of getting me what I want."

16. Men Stay Poor Because They Do Not Realize That Their Entire Success Depends On Who Likes Them.

Your whole financial Future depends on who *likes* you.

If you make life hard for your parents, God will make it hard for you. He said your reaction to your *parents* determines His reaction to your *finances.*

I reached for the phone, called the company, and got the owner. I said, "I really need immediate help. The Spirit of God told me to make these cassettes and get them out to my partners. Can you do that in the next 7 days?"

He said, "Brother Mike, we'd be happy to." That is a guy who makes money. He knows whose joy matters.

Whose joy matters to you? I stress this. Out of everybody in the world, everybody on the earth, all your relatives, everybody you know, one guy, or woman, whoever your boss is, one guy has decided to pay for your Mind. He writes you a check and says, "Thank you for your Mind and your time."

You have relatives. They do not ever write you checks. They ask for checks. But out of everybody, the 6 or 7 billion people on the earth, there is one person that you locked into.

Whoever God Has Allowed To Be Your Boss Is The Divine Secret To Your Prosperity. If it's a woman, or it's a man, it doesn't matter. Whoever gives you instructions is legally, lawfully, *Scripturally, whoever* is the authority over your financial life that gives you instructions at the workplace...I want you here at 9:00. Would you stay here until 6:00? Would you stay here until 7:00? Would you come over to my house and help me for two hours? That is the guy God has authorized to be your Prosperity channel. Do you know that?

Joseph did not sit there in the prison and say, "I *hate* this place. I am getting out of here."

Are you kidding? Joseph performed for the boss over Him. God doesn't circumvent the chain of authority.

God Works Through The Chain of Authority. Whoever is the spiritual authority, financial authority over your *life,* God is continuously looking for somebody to bless.

17. Men Stay Poor Because They Refuse To

Show Honor In Their Employment.

They trivialize the instructions of the man who writes them checks. I am trying to teach that to youth.

I called one day and said, "I need you here at about 1:00pm at my house." At 1:30 I got a phone call.

"Dr. Murdock, we're about to leave The Wisdom Center."

I said, "No, you stay there. You can't even follow the first instruction I gave you. I did not tell you to leave The Wisdom Center at 1:30. I told you to be at my house at 1:00. You can't even follow that instruction? You're the last person I want around my life."

Do you walk in excellence? I ask this with boldness and strength, because I know you can prosper. You can rise to any level of financial blessing you can pick.

Have you found out who is for you? Have you discovered the Divine investment in you? Do you know that you have the Mind of Christ, that you have the strength of God, and the energy of The Holy Spirit? Have you recognized that the God of this entire universe lives inside you and this is your world?

We have been created to rule and to reign. I am talking about the Mind of Christ will be inside of you. I decree that the Mind of Christ will enter you, reign in you and every decision you make will be Prosperity and increase.

I decree a 7-fold return over everything satan has stolen from you all of your whole life must come back to you. Good measure, pushed down, shaken together.

I decree the 100-fold return on every *Seed* that you have ever planted, and every *Seed* that has never come up will get a new schedule from God, and this year you will see the hand of God in everything that you touch. This will be the *happiest* year of your life.

I decree you will walk in *perfect health.* That your house will become debt-free as a testimony of the goodness of God. This is your year for *success.* This is your year for *Prosperity.*

Hold your *Bible* up close and just say these words, "Precious Holy Spirit. I am your protégé. You are my mentor. I trust Your voice. I am addicted to Your presence.

"I will receive a 7-fold return on everything satan has stolen from me.

"I receive new health, new healing in my body, Wisdom for my family, Wisdom on my job. This is my year and I walk in Prosperity. I have Divine energy. I have Divine ideas. In the name of Jesus. Amen and amen."

2

THE 5 TRAPS OF POVERTY

♫ I love sitting at Your feet
I love hearing what You say.
I love knowing Your desires.
I love knowing Your desires.
I am so pleasured to obey.
I am so pleasured to obey.
Your Favor is like sunrise.
Your Favor is like sunrise.
Driving, driving all my nights away.
All my nights away.
I love sitting at Your feet every single day, yes.
I love sitting, I love sitting at Your feet every single day.

Repeat this prayer with me:

"Precious Holy Spirit, You are my Master Mentor. I am a passionate protégé. I love Your Voice. I love Your Presence. I am addicted to Your Presence.

"When You speak, I listen. When You instruct me, I obey. When You correct me, I change.

"I prosper because I hear Your Voice.

"My decisions are Divine decisions.

"Today, I am a Receiver of every Divine gift, every

good and perfect gift. Thank You for the Blood of
Christ. Thank You for the Promise. Thank You for Your
Presence. Today, I receive Uncommon Wisdom and
every decision I make will be a God-decision. In Jesus'
Name." Hallelujah! Hallelujah! Hallelujah!
Hallelujah!

♫ There is nobody, there is nobody like You.
There is nobody, there is nobody like You.
Sweet Holy Spirit, sweet Holy Spirit,
There is nobody, there is nobody like You.
Anything You want, anything You ask,
Whatever You desire, Lord, just name the task.
That is what I will do, oh, that is what I will do.
Precious Holy Spirit, I am in love with You.
I am in love, I am in love, I am in love, I am in love,
I am in love, I am in love, I am in love with You.

*The Difference In People Is Who They Decide To
Pleasure.*
*I Cannot Change Your Life Until I Change Who
You Pleasure.*
The Difference In Seasons Is Who Likes You.
*When You Solve A Problem For Someone, You Prove
Honor.*
*Everywhere You Sow Honor, Favor Becomes The
Fruit of Honor.*
*Favor Is The Fruit From Someone You Have
Honored.*
Everywhere There Is Favor, There Is Prosperity.

♫ I love sitting at Your feet.
I love hearing everything You say.

Whatever You desire, Lord, just name the task.
That is what I will do, oh, that is what I will do
Precious Holy Spirit, I am in love with you.
I'm in love. I'm in love, I'm in love, ah, yes.
I'm in love, I'm in love with You.

Teach me how to please You.
Show me how to pleasure You today.
Let me live in Your presence that comes every time
I obey.

♫ Dominate me with Your Word.
Dominate me with Your Word.
Dominate me with Your Holy Word.
Dominate me with Your Word.
Dominate my Mind with Your Word.
Dominate my Mind with Your Word.
Oh, dominate my Mind with Your Holy Word.
Dominate my Mind with Your Word.
Dominate my house with Your Word.
Dominate my house with Your Word.
Oh, dominate my house with Your Word.
Dominate my house with Your Word.
Dominate my mouth with Your Word.
Dominate my mouth with Your Word.
Dominate my mouth with Your Holy Word.
Dominate my house with Your Word.

When I'm in Your Presence, I change.
I'm just not the same.
I'm just not the same.
When I'm in Your Presence, Holy Spirit, I change.
And I can't go back to yesterday again.

On a Thursday night in my Bible study, I began to weep in my Secret Place. And these words came out.

♫ I'm in love, I'm in love, I'm in love.
I'm in love, I'm in love, I'm in love.
Sweet Holy Spirit, I'm in love.
I'm in love, I'm in love, I'm in love, I'm in love.
I'm in love, I'm in love, I'm in love.
Sweet Holy Spirit, I'm in love. Mm mm mm.

♫ What men take away, God will restore.
And when He gives back, God always gives more,
So never, never fear,
When you lose something you hold dear.
What man takes away,
What man takes away, ah ha,
What man takes away,
My Father always restores.

This is for somebody:
♫ I was broken, now I'm mended again.
I was broken, oh, but now I'm mended again.
And scars just remind me,
God's grace always finds me.
I was broken, now I'm mended again.

Hallelujah. Hallelujah. Hallelujah. I feel like writing a song.

I'm a walking Miracle.

Why do not you just say that: I'm a walking Miracle.

Go ahead. Put a real cocky look on your face. "I'm a walking Miracle."

If somebody comes to you and says, "I do not believe in Miracles."

Say, "Don't you believe in me? I am a walking Miracle."

Ah, say that out loud: "I am a walking Miracle. *I am a walking Miracle.*"

Dr. Mike Smalley is normally traveling all over the world and we are so glad to have him visiting with us. He has started over 60 churches around the world. And he is a true, true servant of the Lord. Praise God.

Dr. Mike Smalley: As I have been praying this last few weeks, The Holy Spirit has really been impressing upon me something that Dr. Murdock even mentioned and that is the importance *of becoming addicted to the Voice of The Holy Spirit* and training yourself over and over – nobody talks more than the Lord.

But He talks in different ways and understanding that sometimes one of the last things He uses is words.

He speaks *through nudges and inner persuasions.*

He speaks *through the removal of His peace.*

He speaks *through of course people.*

He speaks *through His Word.*

But really *train* yourself to sit at His feet and to be *sensitive* that He is always for you and He is always speaking.

He is *always guiding.*

He is *always moving.*

Be very sensitive to a moment that changes within your heart. Sometimes you will go to do something and everything seems to be okay and in order, and you will have an inner nudge *that something's just not right now.* This is not it.

Pay attention to those. Train yourself on those, and expect the Lord to lead you We have had some things happen in our office the last few days. People contacting us from years back that we hadn't heard from in years and hearing the testimonies of what the Lord had done in crusades and meetings and, and even conversations. These were things that we'd all forgotten about, but realize now that the Lord was working *behind* the scenes.

I am convinced, The Holy Spirit wants to bring things back from our past. Not the sin part, not the failures but He'll arrange Divine appointments.

You'll have days you think, *I am not impacting anybody, I have not had a success in these areas.* And then The Holy Spirit will bring something back and show you that there was an impact there you did not yet know about, you hadn't seen or that it had multiplied in effect. So watch for that.

So when you stay addicted to His Voice, when you walk – I will never forget, I was in the hospital years ago visiting someone and felt a leading from the Lord to go a different direction — to actually take some stairs instead of the elevator. I did. I came upon the floor and ran into two people I did not know, but they knew me.

Someone was there that had cancer, that needed healing, and I was able to go minister to them. The husband accepted Christ in the hospital room. He was not saved. His wife had cancer.

All of that because I took the stairs and not an elevator. So you pay attention to the inner promptings of The Holy Spirit because He has something special for all of us. God bless you.

Dr. Mike Murdock: I am a man who believes in

blessing. It is part of the Bible.

Which part of the Bible *have you decided to ignore?*

Which part of the Bible *have you decided to magnify?*

Life Is Whatever You Decide To Magnify In Your Mind.

God Gave Us A Mind To Resize Experiences.

I am the only one who can determine, decide and choose what's important to me.

Some of you have made the accusations and the criticism of your enemies, more important than your own opinion.

Somebody tweeted me one time after they'd criticized me, "I hope I did not hurt you."

I said, "Had your opinion mattered, it would have. I consider my opinion as valuable as anybody else's."

I consider my opinion as valuable as anybody else's, and so should you. Some of you are upset because somebody criticized you.

Doesn't your own opinion matter to you?

Doesn't your opinion of you matter more than an adversary?

Somebody jumps all over you and then says, "Oh, I hope I did not hurt you."

Say, "Had your opinion mattered, it would have."

Say, "I have the Mind of Christ. I have the power of God, and greater is He that is within me than he that is within the world."

Proverbs 4:7-8 says, "Wisdom is the principal thing; therefore get Wisdom: and with all thy getting get understanding. Exalt her, and she shall promote thee: she shall bring thee to honour, when thou dost embrace her."

What is Wisdom?
Wisdom Is The Ability To Recognize Difference.
Difference *in an environment.*
Difference *between right and wrong.*

The purpose of Wisdom is to decide, discern, recognize difference between an evil person and a right person. (Read Proverbs 2:12, 16.)

Difference in an environment.
Difference in a moment.
Difference in an opportunity.
Your difference from another.
Somebody else's difference from you.
Wisdom Is The Ability To Recognize Difference In Value.

I was buying some gold yesterday and I said, "Now, why is this more valuable than this?"

"Well, this is backed by the U.S. government, but this is backed by the companies that get the gold and engrave it."

Everything has a difference.

The Purpose of Wisdom Is To Discern Who Should Be Honored.

Remember: *The Difference Between Success And Failure Is Who You Honor.*

If you fail with your life, I will ask you, "Who did you choose to dishonor? Who have you refused to Honor?"

If out of your 5 children, two choose to Honor you; those are the two that you should Honor. *To Honor Is The Rewarding of Someone For Their Difference.*

Remember to continuously *listen* for difference.

You listen for difference in a conversation.
You listen for pain.

You listen for information.

Always listen for the sound of Honor because...*It is Impossible To Improve Anybody's Life Until You Change Who They Honor.*

You will be forced to live with dishonor. If you are not careful, you can allow somebody's dishonor to diminish and dismantle your ability to Honor. *Someone's dishonoring you is not permission for you to dishonor them.*

The Role of Wisdom Is To Recognize Who You Should Honor.

I think that is the chief fruit of Wisdom.

If I know who you have chosen to Honor, I can measure your Wisdom.

I want to hear how a child *talks* to their mother.

I want to hear how a son *reacts* to his father, so I can predict his Future.

That is the role of Wisdom.

Poverty is a trap.

Poverty *destroys* freedom of choice.

Poverty destroys options.

The major reason for Financial Prosperity is to create experiences for you and for other people.

The father who is prosperous can create the experience of a safe house in a safe neighborhood for his children.

A young mother, if she is prosperous, can buy the car that takes her to her job. She's able to come back home and prepare a meal that blesses her family. She can buy her children clothes that stop them from feeling ashamed and embarrassed in front of others.

The greatest mistake possibly you will make in your life is to trivialize Financial Prosperity.

Religious people have been taught to *ignore* it because it's the weapon that causes Christianity to go around the world.

A Christian without money is almost without influence. The Bible says there is a man in the Bible who had great Wisdom. He understood the strategy for their city, but because he had no money, no one would listen to him.

Psalm 112:1-3, "Praise ye the Lord. Blessed is the man that feareth the Lord, that delighteth greatly in His commandments. His Seed shall be mighty upon earth: the generation of the upright shall be blessed. Wealth and riches shall be in his house: and his righteousness endureth for ever."

Twenty percent of what Christ talked about was money.

Was Jesus poor? Of course not.

He said, "The poor you have with you always but not Me."

Was Jesus poor? One of His 12 did nothing but carry a bag of money.

Was Jesus poor? He said to them, when His disciples saw a little prostitute use two years of her income to pour perfume on His feet, "And in sorrow washed His feet and dried His feet with her long hair," (read Matthew 26:8-10).

His disciple says, "This could have been used to help the poor."

So even His disciples did not think He was poor.

Deuteronomy 28:1 says, "And it shall come to pass, if thou shalt hearken diligently unto the voice of the Lord thy God, to observe and to do all His commandments."

Notice "if...if...if." This means *Prosperity is a human decision.* It is a Divine provision, but it's a human decision.

One of the great purposes of Wisdom is to distinguish between God's decision for my life and my decision for my life.

There are 331 references in the Bible similar to Isaiah 1:19 says, "If ye be willing and obedient, ye shall eat the good of the land." *If* I am willing and obedient.

Prosperity requires qualification.

Divine love requires no qualification.

I do not have to do anything to become loved. But, I have to do something to become blessed.

The blessings of the Lord are *unrelated* to His Love.

His Love toward me is the same to everybody in the world, that is why I did not feel so special when I found out God loved everybody else too.

When I found out He loves Saddam Hussein, and Osama Bin Laden.

I said, "Shoot, I would like to get into a new level where God likes me."

God does not bless me because He loves me.

He loves me because I need Him, but He blesses me because I obey Him.

The Blessing of the Lord requires my *obedience* to a law.

The Law of Adaptation. Dinosaurs no longer exist on the earth because they could not adapt, but cockroaches have been on the earth for millions of years because they could adapt.

The Law of Focus. Thomas Edison, the famous inventor, said many people think that I am smarter than other men but I am not. He said my difference from other men is very simple. He said other men think of many things all day long but I think of only *one thing* all day long.

Imagine your success if your entire thought life was focused on one thing. All of your ideas was on one thing.

How do you kill a man with an idea? Give him 10 more. How do you kill a man with a dream? Give him a second one. *The Only Reason Men Fail Is Broken Focus.*

In Deuteronomy 28:1 God is saying, what will happen if I respond to His word? If...if...if. "...if thou shalt hearken diligently unto the voice of the Lord thy God, to observe and to do all His commandments which I command thee this day, that the Lord thy God will set thee on high above all nations of the earth."

The passion to excel is Divine.

The passion to surpass another is Divine.

Rivalry is Divine.

Competition is Divine.

God said if you do this, this is what will happen. If you do not, this is what will happen.

The passion for increase came from God. It is not satanic. How do we know that? Before Adam and Eve ever failed, before they ever sinned, the serpent looked at Adam and Eve and said, "If you partake of this fruit, you will know more, you will be like a god, you will excel." They had never sinned. They had never tasted rebellion. They had never fallen. Yet this passion to excel and do better and increase, this desire for a second house is not demonic. This desire for a second car is not demonic.

Jesus said in John 10:10, "The thief cometh not, but for to steal, and to kill, and to destroy: I am come that they might have life, and that they might have it more abundantly."

God even uses increase as an incentive and a reward system for obedience. He said if I do this, I will cause you to increase.

In Deuteronomy 1:11, He says if it was up to Me, I wish you were a thousand times more. In Mark 10:28-30, He tells Peter, anything that you give up for Me will come back to you 100-fold.

Malachi 3:10, He said if my Offering and my Tithe would accompany my prayer, then the windows of Heaven would open because of my Tithe, and my prayers would enter the Heavens and that is the purpose of opening up Heaven so my prayers accompanying my Tithe will be heard by God. It is my Offering that opens up the windows of Heaven, so my prayers can be heard in Divine Presence.

Then He proceeds to talk about The Blessing. Deuteronomy 28:2-4, "And all these blessings shall come on thee, and overtake thee, if thou shalt hearken unto the voice of the Lord thy God. Blessed shalt thou be in the city, and blessed shalt thou be in the field. Blessed shall be the fruit of thy body, and the fruit of thy ground..." And then He talks about suddenly I am going to cause all your animals to want to make love and reproduce. You're going to have the most loving animals you have ever seen. He said the cattle are going to increase. The sheep are going to increase.

Look at verse 8, "The Lord shall command the blessing upon thee in thy storehouses." What does that mean? That means *excess.* What you do not need right now. What you do not need for yourself. I am going to give you some extra in case you have got some slow-moving friends that need to be blessed.

The blessing of the Lord is not a Divine decision. It is a Divine *desire.* It is a Divine *design.* He is the Divine Source, but the amount of my blessing is proportionate to my obedience.

5 Traps of Poverty:

1.   The Trap of Inferiority. Do you feel like you are not *good* enough? Do you feel like you do not *deserve* it? You will notice that those who do not dress well, those that do not have money, if they are not angry and vindictive, there is a sense of inferiority. I am not good enough. I am not accustomed to this. My momma had no money. My daddy has no money.

You will always hear somebody in poverty trapped in this self-portrait of a victim. I am a victim. *Why are you poor?* Because my daddy 200 years ago, my granddaddy 200 years ago had his house stolen from him.

Why are you poor? Because my momma gave me no money. My daddy had no money.

Why are you poor? Because I did not get to go to college. Why did not you get to go to college? I had no money. Why do you want me to drive you everywhere? Because I can't buy a car. Why can't you buy a car? I do not have any money.

That is a trap, and you start seeing yourself like a victim. I have nothing. I can't do anything. Because of them.

Poverty is a spirit. It is not a financial level, it's a spirit that comes on your life. When you talk about what you do not have instead of what you do have.

You got two eyes? But I can't go see anything because we can't afford to go on vacation because we do not have no money."

You got hands? "Yeah, but I can't buy a manicure because I do not have any money."

Self-portrait is deadly. *The way you see you is as valuable as the way you see God.* How do I know that? From Numbers 13:32-33. When the 10 of the 12 spies says, "We are like grasshoppers next to them." *Never compare your weakness with somebody else's gift.* Never study your weakness, study your *Difference.*

The first thing God will do when He wants to prosper you is change the way you see you.

Women act different from day to day. If it's a bad hair day it is a witch hazel day. When a woman's hair is not falling in place, and she knows when it's not, and she thinks everybody else knows. You know how she acts. But when a woman feels good looking, "Hello world. I am here."

How do you see you? Do you realize you are the offspring of the Most High God? Have you realized that God has invested something in you that nobody else has? Have you found your Divine Difference from your family? Have you found the secret investment that God has stored in you that nobody else has even recognized? Do you *magnify* your difference or your weakness?

"Brother Mike, I just feel inferior to everybody. Everybody's better looking than me." There is something you have been given. Say this sentence aloud. "Nobody else has what God has put in me. *I break the trap of inferiority.*"

2. The Trap of Resentment. Do you resent the blessed?

I see it happening in our government right now. Everybody's arguing who should pay the most taxes. Well, I only make $25,000, I shouldn't pay 10 percent. I shouldn't pay 15 percent because I do not have any money. That guy's got a lot of money, he should pay my bills. He should pay for my insurance. He should pay for my car.

You ignoramus. Did Jesus take from the man with 5 talents? Did He take from the man with 5 and say, "This man over here is really feeling bad because he only has one talent?" *No!* (Read Matthew 25:26-30.) He looked at the man with one and said, "You little rat, I am going to take the one talent you have and give it to the guy whose working his 5."

I like George Foreman. He told his momma, "Momma, some day I am going to buy you a nice house." They would pass by and see the house in Houston on a hill the he admired. His father was not a good parent. He had a rough situation. But he admired achievers. He did not resent them. He did not say, "Who do you think you are?"

I used to want to bring my Rolls Royce to the church, because I wanted to show it off. Just let everybody know I had bought a Rolls Royce.

When I bought it, it was a huge, big thing because I would always admire people who owned a Rolls Royce. Then I noticed that so many young people would look for nice cars in the parking lot and they would, what they call "key" them. They would take a car key and scrape the car, and there is a $40,000.00 paint job bill to pay. So you had to have somebody out there to guard your car.

If I hear the sound of resentment in you over

somebody who has something you do not have, I know there is no possibility of you succeeding.

Read the success stories and the biographies of successful people, which I do. If you want to lose weight, do you find somebody weighing 350 pounds and say talk to me about losing weight?

If I want a financial blessing on my life, do I go to somebody who lost their house last week? *Never resent the blessed.* Learn from the blessed. How did you get what you got? How did it happen? Tell me the story. Give me the secrets. Who do you learn from? Who are you willing to learn from? Who have you invested time to learn from?

A friend of mine called me and he says, "Dr. Peter J. Daniels wants to meet with you for a few hours. But he is in Austin. He is flying in from Australia."

I knew Dr. Peter J. Daniels. We're friends. He was an illiterate bricklayer from Australia. He could not read nor write but he got saved under Billy Graham's ministry and when he got saved, God taught him to read and write. He read 7,000 biographies and became a billionaire.

So when Dr. Robb Thompson said, "Would you like to meet with him?" I said, "I am flying in another direction," but we turned and we went the other direction. I sat for 4 hours at the table. Why? He knows something I do not know. He sees something I do not see. He feels what I do not feel. He has something I do not have.

Somebody who has something you do not have has discovered something you ought to know. *Your Pursuit Qualifies You To Receive.* Your *unwillingness* to ask *disqualifies* you. I want to see the list of your questions.

One of my close friends is a cardiologist in Pittsburgh. He has 40 different offices. He wants to open up one here in Dallas. He is one of my strongest supporters and investors in our ministry. He always has a table spread for me at Cornerstone Television so when I get there, he knows I love Asian food, Indian food, and so he always has a big buffet...more than I could eat for a week.

So he is driving me back to my hotel so we'd have some time to eat and talk. He has 67,000 patients... 67,000 patients. He begins to talk to me about New York and he said, "I believe there is something for you in New York." He said, "Think about it. Think about it. Twenty-five million people in a 100-mile radius." He says, "In New York, there is a global voice."

I said, "Talk to me about my health. I want to get healthy." As he began to talk, I began to document. He knows something I do not know. He began to describe the 3 major health problems among Americans. The top 3 reasons people die can be traced to the food we eat.

The most important thing you will do every day of your life is ask questions. Ask questions of yourself. Ask questions of others. Ask questions of The Holy Spirit.

Who do you resent and why? I see great resentment and hostility toward the Prosperity message, as the man who tweeted me said, "I watched you on TV. You talked for one hour about money. Why?" I tweeted him back, "The same reason you work 40 hours to get some." Fortunately fools never remain hidden.

Who do you resent? Why? One of the traps of poverty is the trap of resentment of those who have unlocked the secrets, those who have plenty, those who have Prosperity. I see it in the sneer. I see it in the words.

I saw it when one of the Presidential candidates felt *embarrassed* for saying he was worth 250 million dollars. And the other was *thankful* that he had no money so he could appear *humble.* Do you think I want a *poor* man in the White House who could be *bought* with a single check?

Who do you resent and why? The Trap of Resentment will *suffocate* your ability to learn. *You Cannot Learn From Somebody You Resent.*

Look at what we do for foreign countries and Third World countries. I do not care if it's Haiti or Afghanistan or Pakistan. Look at the resentment of The United States.

They do not meet us so they can ask us what they could do differently? How we could change our country? They say, "Give us 5 billion. If you give us 5 billion we will let you have a Navy here, let you have Marines here."

The poor often have a resentment. I can hear it in Christianity.

3. The Trap of Permission. We *permit* ourselves to be poor. We *authorize* ourselves by finding something good about being poor.

Even Mother Teresa said God must *love* poor people, He made so *many.* God must love fleas, He made so many. My interpretation of that statement is, God must love fleas. God must love snakes since He made so many. God must love demon spirits since He made so many.

Over the centuries, through the Roman Catholic

Church and church governments, there has been an attitude toward the poor, not just to *help* them, but to *keep* them poor.

The poor end up like the child that finds out that when he or she is sick, her father will hold her and cradle her. The father will say, "Baby, are you sick? I will get you some candy." Well, she's learning. "I do not feel good." "Oh, baby, let's buy you some candy. Let daddy hold you."

Attention is a craving. Attention is a passion. So we bring the poor to a place of reliability on the wealthy. Wanting handouts; with a "take care of me" mentality.

I am not talking about people who have been in horrible tragic tsunamis and earthquakes, and people who have never been trained and taught to prosper. I am talking about the mindset that says, I permit myself to be *poor* and to be *sponsored* by everybody else.

I permit myself not to prosper.

I think it is ludicrous to be out of a job for two years. Everywhere there is a problem, there is a job. That is all a job is...solving a problem. So when you tell me, I *cannot* find a job, you are telling me I do not see *any* problems to solve on the earth.

Would you want to hire somebody that can't see a problem? *Have you given yourself permission to have nothing?* Have you given yourself permission to live without a house? To live without a car? Have you given permission to others to take care of you?

My father used to walk independently, then people started coming alongside him to help him. I was glad they did, but suddenly my father started walking with a bit of a hunch.

Have you permitted yourself to have nothing?

Have you permitted yourself to adjust and adapt to a life of poverty? Well, some have it and some do not. That is a trap. It is a Mind trap. The willingness to do without. I hate poverty. I see nothing good in poverty.

"Brother Mike, money won't make you happy." And how would you know? Money's an exciting thing. May this church never hear those phrases, "Money is not important."

Well, your ear isn't hearing, let's just cut it off, you do not Mind. You know what, you have two arms, let's just cut one of them off because you are just sitting anyway.

I want you to know, we have a Jehovah-jireh that wants us blessed. He said, Matthew 7:11, "If ye then, being evil, know how to give good gifts unto your children, how much more shall your Father which is in Heaven give good things to them that ask Him?"

What man is not excited when his little girl finds something she loves? I love it when someone I love finds something they like. I am excited.

4. The Trap of Isolation. When you feel ashamed...or embarrassed, you isolate from other people. You stop talking to other people. You say, "I have to do this thing by myself. I am going to be independent of everybody."

I remember my son one time said, "I want to run away from home." He said, "I do not want to depend on anybody."

I said, "How are you going to get to the airport?"

He said, "The taxi."

I said, "No, you have to live by yourself. You have to be independent now, you have to get to the airport by yourself."

"Well," he said, "I will walk."

I said, "Then when you get to the airport, do you want anybody to fly you?"

God made us *interdependent on each other.* Don't try to live isolated - you will go nuts trying to live without the feedback of others. People talking into your spirit. Talking into your heart. People advising you.

A friend of mine called me from New York. He has been going through the worst year of his life.

I inquired, "What does your circle of council say?"

I said, "God instructed preachers to have 7 people who would advise them. Seven people who would give them advice. One person can't see everything. You can't drink enough carrot juice to see behind your head. If I look north, I can't see south. If I look west, I can't see east. Everybody sees something you do not see."

He said, "Well, I have a couple of friends but they do not return my phone calls."

I said, "Who is your circle of 7? Who is your circle of encouragement?"

Your life has circles of people. I have people and I code them. A circle of comfort. Who's voice *comforts* you when a storm is there?

Have you identified people who *inspire* you? I can't live without inspiration. There are days I do not want to get up at all. There are days I do not see a great reason to get up. Something's happened in my emotions...my Mind. Maybe my Mind took a problem and made it so big that all I think about is my problem. My life is just one big mess of problems. So I have to have a circle of inspiration.

Whose voice inspires you? There are people in your life whose voice agitates you. They do not have to show up; all you need to do is hear their voice.

There are others whose voice *unlocks* something in you. Don't isolate yourself in your poverty and think that you are in this battle alone. Believe it or not, there are two or 3 people that would be ecstatic if they saw you drive up in a Mercedes and they'd say, "Wow, oh, you have a Mercedes."

"Yeah, but Mike, I have another person that gets upset every time I..." We're not talking about that circle. We're talking about the circle of encouragers.

I called Dr. Dan Tyler, the President of International Seminary, when I was going through a real Mind-battle in my life. I just could not see anything good in my life for weeks and weeks. I was so obsessed with correcting people who would not change.

God's been able to get on with His life since one-third of His angels became fools. Now, how would you like to be God? Wake up one morning and one out of every 3 people around you was stupid. Now, you say, "Well, yeah, He could throw them to the earth and get rid of them. There is nobody I can throw over to Mars or Venus."

God was able to see one out of 3 angels rebel against His character but He said, "I am going to do something new." Hallelujah. Hallelujah. "I am going to do a new thing."

A girl tweeted me some weeks ago, "Dr. Mike, my boyfriend has nothing to do with me anymore. And he won't take me out." And so I tweeted her back, *"Rejection Is An Opportunity For Divine Replacement."*

When God lets somebody walk out of your life, He has arranged for the next level to move in to your life. Hallelujah. Don't isolate because somebody talked to you bad. Don't isolate because somebody embarrassed you.

I am real touched by the bullying thing that goes on in our schools and there are so many children that deal with criticism. Children can hurt children. There is this increase of suicides among teenagers now and it's a deadly thing.

Let's say you are poor. You can hardly make ends meet. Start with what you have. I do not think poor people inventory their Divine investment. I think they look at what they do not have instead of what they do have.

Let's start with some opportunities. Who likes you? Who wants to know you? Who's giving you an opportunity to work? Show your Difference.

5. The Trap of Insignificance. Everywhere there is a problem, there is money. Everywhere. A problem is an invitation to Prosperity. Until you solve a problem, nobody needs you. *If somebody doesn't have a problem, you are unnecessary.* When you *see* a problem and you *solve* it, you create Divine debt. God now owes you.

"Brother Mike, I work hard for my boss and he doesn't even notice me. He is not even there."

So you do not believe God's everywhere? So who are you working for? If you will become the master problem-solver in your environment. Listen for a problem.

Your mom said, "I hate making these beds." You just got an invitation. "Momma, you should never have to make a bed the rest of your life. I will make my bed, and I will make your bed. Momma, show me how."

You getting it? "Momma, I not only will make my

bed, I am going to make yours too. How would you like it made? Momma, teach me how to make it."

When you decide to be a problem-solver, the entire universe flows in your Favor. *Problem-solvers create Favor.* Not problem creators.

When you solve a problem, *not create one,* God becomes *indebted* to you. Ephesians 6:8, "Any good thing I do for another I receive from the Lord."

When somebody walks up to me and says, "I want to solve a problem for you." Do you have any idea what that does for me?

There are two statements that have changed my life: *God Leaves No Man Unrewarded,* and *No Good Man Will Leave Anybody Unrewarded.*

I want you to remember something very simple. *Money is not a Miracle.* There is nothing wrong with praying for Favor; remember that money is not a Miracle nor Mystery.

Money Is A Very Simple Reward System.

When You Solve A Problem, You Prove Honor.

Everywhere You Show Honor, You Create Favor.

Everywhere There Is Favor, There Is Money.

Money is anywhere there is Favor. Even bad people bless people who show Honor. Wrong people even demonstrate Favor. It is a Divine Law.

Just look for a problem to solve.

Years ago an evangelist called me. He was crying on the phone. He had 5 children. He said, "There is freezing weather. My children have no clothes. I have no place to preach. Would you recommend me to some pastors to create an open door for my ministry?"

I sat down at the First Assembly of God Church in the Sunday School room and handwrote 27 letters to 27 pastors and said, "Would you have my friend Larry for a crusade? He is going through a trial." He received 27 letters...*27 invitations.*

He never sent me a dollar thank you. He never wrote me a thank you. He never sent any money. But The One I work for has kept a thousand doors open everywhere around the world. A thousand-plus doors that I could drop in any nation in the world. What I made happen for him, God made happen for me. *What You Make Happen For Others, God Makes Happen For You.*

Listen for the sound of a *problem.* Stop when you hear the sound of *pain.* Everywhere there is pain, there is a profit. P-R-O-F-I-T. I mean reward. *Everywhere There Is A Problem, There Is A Profit.*

A young man decided that the little nano Mp3 Player that Apple had created could be a watch, and that you could put pictures on it and add other features. He went to Apple and they said, "No, our product was not made to be a watch. Our nano player is not for that."

So he went online and said, "I need $15,000.00 to create a prototype of this. If you invest $50.00 in my little company I am starting to make these, I will give you a free watch band to go with it when I come out with it." Instead of $15,000.00, he has $963,000.00 to create a little watch. Of course, now Apple says, "We have a revelation and we want to participate."

Do you realize how many problems are on the earth? Do you realize that the earth is full of problems? Problems make you important. Until somebody has a problem, you do not get a salary.

Problems Are Invitations To Significance.

Invitations to document your difference. I have a lot of problems in my life, so everywhere there is a problem, there is the potential for a reward system.

I believe this with all my heart. I love to tell this little illustration. Years ago, I walked out of my hotel room and went downstairs to the lobby. A man yelled out my name.

I said, "Yes." I walked over.

He says, "I have wanted to meet you." I had never heard of him. I did not know him, but I talked to him. He said, "My business has a major problem. I do not have enough money – I am going to go bankrupt if there is not something."

My first thought was, "Well, let's just pray." Remember, if you just pray for somebody, that is one thing. But there is another kind of way to help. And I said, "Maybe I can help you."

"No, no, no." And he begin to name all the consultants and people he had and none of them had made a difference.

I said, "Let me fly in and let me participate. Let me just be a part of it."

He said, "It is way beyond that."

I said, "I am free. I own a jet. I have two pilots. And I will zip in and do it for free." I said, "You can't beat free." I will go to a store to get free cat food even though I do not have a cat. I said, "I am free."

He said, "Would you need to be there about two weeks?"

I said, "No, just a couple of hours."

He calls me a few weeks later and he says, "I do not know how to thank you. But the least I could do is give you $130,000.00." When he said that, I thought,

"Whoa! What's the most he can do if that is the least he can do?" And he gave me $130,000.00.

I remember the day a man asked me if I would speak to his leaders. Pastor Monica said, "He wants to know what your honorarium is." I said, "Oh, I do not have an honorarium, I am free."

God is so World-Class that I do not want somebody lower class deciding my experiences. God is so World-Class, I do not want an unclassy person deciding my reward system. I want God deciding my reward system. So I told him I would do it for free.

When I came off the platform, the man had tears in his eyes. He said, "I have never done anything like this in my life. I have had this Rolex watch, it's a very special expensive watch, would you, would you be willing to receive this as a gift?"

I said, "Oh, brother, I am a master Receiver. Absolutely I will receive that as a gift." And then two weeks later, in comes an appreciation blessing for me in an envelope. "Thank you for changing my company, blessing my leaders, and" (he gave me an extra tip, above the Rolex watch just to tip me a little extra) "here's $100,000.00. Thanking you."

I live by this law. I am in Partnership with The Most High God.

❧ **3** ❧

YOUR ASSIGNMENT WILL REQUIRE PROSPERITY

Prosperity Is Not Only Important, But Necessary.

Prosperity is necessary for you to be able to fulfill a command from God...an Assignment.

A lot of people simply want a Miracle, and Wisdom is not their focus. They want to get out of a problem but they do not know how they got in it so they will stay in the problem.

Through the years of my life I have wanted to know why bad things happen. *How can they be avoided?*

The purpose of The Word of God is to help us *avoid* pain and *create* pleasurable seasons in our life. The Bible is a "how-to" book of how to avoid painful seasons.

▶ How to *get along with God.*

▶ How to *become an Overcomer.*

▶ How to *develop the nature of a Warrior.*

▶ How to *have skilled conversation with God.*

The Bible is a book on how to *discover* your Assignment. God gave you your Assignment when you were in your mother's womb.

I am not trying to address why tsunamis have wiped out cities and countries. I am not attempting to explain why earthquakes decimate areas, or explain why you have an accident and are in a coma for 3 months.

This book is dedicated to exploring *Why Men Stay Poor.* We believe in the miraculous intervention of God, but I want to help you understand why people live in lack.

Resentment Aborts Learning. If I resent somebody successful, I cannot learn from them.

I want to address the financial part of Prosperity. The financial zones of our life are normally avoided by religion. Religion teaches men to *adapt* to poverty, to *accept* poverty as a part of the plan of God. We try to divert a lot of it by saying things like, "You can be happy without a new car."

Religion says you can be happy without a house. You can be happy without an ear, a nose, or a wife. You can be happy if a happy moment is all you are looking for.

But if you have an obsession to *pleasure* the heart of God, money will become important to you. If you have compassion for people, money will become *significant* to you.

I am not talking about the guy that hires 100 people, or even 5,000 people. I am not speaking of a GE or a Wal-Mart that may hire 300,000 or 800,000 employees.

I am talking about the heart that wants to create good experiences for people. When Bishop Saúl González walked me through the huge trash dump area of Puerto Vallarta, Mexico, with Linda Knight, a lady minister from Seattle, Washington, my compassion was stirred. These leaders were all important to my life.

Linda and her husband Joe were precious to me. Linda said "Dr. Mike, look at these people. Look at these kids." They were digging through the trash cans, trying to find a banana peel to eat so they could survive.

The Bishop was a great man who went to be with the Lord. I told his son a few weeks ago while he was here from Mexico at The Wisdom Center, "We're standing by you like we stood by your father. As long as I am alive, or until Jesus comes, I will pay for the food for these thousands of children out there in the dump."

Since then he has built a School of Champions for these young people. They are growing up now, getting into high school. They told me the other day one of them is becoming a politician. That is how many years we have been supporting and standing with them.

It is big to me. It is huge to me.

Lindy McCauley is one of God's choice queens on the earth. She is a magnificent woman of God. She brought a young couple along with her to visit me. With tears in her eyes she said, "We have a lot of children in South Africa who have been orphaned by AIDS. Both parents died because of AIDS."

They told me about 3 little boys. I met the little boys when I went to Johannesburg. One of them clung to me and went to sleep on my shoulder.

I love God through loving people. They found the little boys in trash heaps and wrecked automobiles. I believe anything I do for a human is something I have done for God. *Anything You Do For A Human, You Have Done For God.*

They said, "Would you underwrite The Home of Hope?"

I agreed that I would underwrite all of their food, medical expenses, teachers and their clothing. I would do everything I could except be there. I promised to hire a staff, and we did.

That is *The Mike Murdock Home of Hope* in Johannesburg. Why? We have a calling. *We are Deliverers.*

Isaiah 61 made it very clear that there are deliverers, and there are captives. We have a calling. I have a passion to *remove* pain on the earth.

I am not called to everybody. I am called to somebody, and I seine the ocean of humanity to find the people that I am called to.

When you seine the ocean, you put a net through the ocean, and you get some fish. Sometimes you catch a snake. Sometimes there are crabs. Sometimes there are things you do not want or like, but that is part of the netting.

Our obsession is *finding* people that we can help. We want to identify those we can *heal,* and we can pour the oil of God on.

Everyone Has A Different Calling.

I am not mad at my banker because he doesn't mow my grass. My ear is not my eye. My eye doesn't sneer sarcastically at my ear and say, "You just sit there the whole day and I have to look at everything. If I would have been on that side of the fence I would have seen the baseball coming."

No, they have a *different* function. One of the things that I feel like the Lord has anointed me to do is to *unlock a Partnership* between the Heavenly Father and the Body of Christ.

God is more than just God...He is our Provider. He is the Master Source for every good thing. *God passionately wants to be trusted.* Do you know that? Do you understand that?

I often say that the most important Scripture in your Bible is Numbers 23:19, "God is not a man, that He should lie; neither the son of man, that He should repent: hath He said, and shall He not do it?"

There are *many* reasons men are poor. There is not *one* reason somebody is poor, but you must *hate* poverty.

1.   Some Men Are Poor Because They Have A Wrong View of God. They believe that God has predestined their circumstances. They have been taught that they *have* nothing because God *gave* them nothing.

Jesus taught multiplication and was agitated incredibly by the man with one talent that refused to multiply. He honored the man with 5 who increased what he had.

This is the opposite of the way that our government has chosen to run The United States. Right now The United States is operating under a philosophy that is contrary to Scripture. Jesus did not say the man who has 5 talents should be stripped.

Jesus did not say the man who had produced, multiplied, and increased, should have what he had worked hard to gain stripped. Our government today would take from the successful man and give it to the man with one talent who refused to work, refused to develop himself, and refused to multiply his assets.

I assess everything through Biblical eyes. I do not trust humanity, but I trust The Voice of the Spirit of

God.

The Anointing You Respect Is The Anointing That Increases.

There are many types of anointing. Exodus talks about a man who was anointed to work with silver, and anointed to work with gold.

We have a young lady here at The Wisdom Center who is just remarkable in her ability to paint. I want her to do my greeting cards. Her colors are spectacular. You do not forget what she puts together. *That is a gift.*

To me, it's easy to play the piano. Anybody can play the piano. All the notes are always the same, C, D, E, F, G.

Poverty can turn into Prosperity.

Poverty Is Not A Divine Decision.

Poverty Is A Human Decision.

There are children of impoverished people that have no "say-so." But as they learn and grow, they can *break* generational curses. That is one of the things I want to do in your life is break any generational curse over you. This is especially true where you have had the philosophy that God loves poor people *more* than He loves rich people.

Let's break the philosophy that poverty has its place, and the purpose of the rich people is to sponsor the poor.

I believe it is wise to give to the poor, to bless the poor. There is a blessing attached to giving to the poor, not only financial, but especially physically.

In Psalm 41 and Isaiah 58 we see that every Seed that you plant has a different Future.

Every Seed That You Plant Creates Different Fruit.

The Seed I plant depends on what I have. *The*

Quality of The Soil Determines The Future of Your Seed.

"Mike, if I sow into somebody who is bad soil, will God bless it anyway?"

No. That is the whole point. If God blessed me anyway if I sowed in *bad* soil, what would be the reward for finding *good* soil?

Jesus made that very clear. He answered it without a doubt. He said if I sow where there is stony ground...if I sow among the *thorns,* my Seed is *choked.* He even talks about people that are very excited when they sow and in a few days they are burned. They declare, "Everything was wasted."

Then Jesus talked about *good* soil. Right now I *look* for good soil, and when I *find* good soil, I *sow* a part of me there.

You Are A Walking Seed.

We are going to talk about that, because *poor* people *think* they have *nothing.* I know. I was poor.

A poor person does not think they have enough to become more. *Poor people think poor thoughts.* The ones who stop thinking thoughts of poverty break the generational curse of poverty.

I do not know of anything good in being poor. Some say, "I had nothing, and because of it I learned to enjoy a can instead of buying a toy."

Well, that is wonderful. But if you begin to get blessed – *and that was sarcastic* – you are going to want to bless others.

You are going to want to really make a difference with your sowing. You are going to want to choose where you sow very, very carefully.

Psalm 112:1-3, "Blessed is the man that feareth the Lord, that delighteth greatly in His commandments. His Seed shall be mighty upon earth: the generation of the upright shall be blessed. Wealth and riches shall be in his house: and his righteousness endureth for ever."

He goes on, "Unto the upright there ariseth light in the darkness: he is gracious, and full of compassion, and righteous. A good man sheweth favour, and lendeth: he will guide his affairs with discretion. Surely he shall not be moved for ever: the righteous shall be in everlasting remembrance. He shall not be afraid of evil tidings: his heart is fixed, trusting in the Lord. His heart is established, he shall not be afraid, until he sees his desire upon his enemies."

When Moses had Korah and 249 of his leaders come against him, he was so agitated God opened up the earth and swallowed all of them. The next day, 14,000 Israelites came against Moses, and God burned all of them to death.

There are times that I want to see the desire of God on my enemies. Recently, I was praying about two people that have really tried to destroy and discredit my life. They have done the most horrifying things I think anybody could do, publishing lies and things meant to stain me.

People Who Are Unmoved By Truth Have To Be Moved By Pain. I asked The Holy Spirit to give them a violent end so that their network of people can cry out in repentance to God for what they have done wrong. I really believe that.

There are people that do not learn. The Bible says their ways will *correct* them.

There are people who are *unmoved* by a Billy Graham sermon. There are people who are unmoved by television teaching and ministry. They *sneer* at pastors and their churches. They *laugh* at the Bible. They are *sarcastic* on television and they act like the Bible is one big joke while they make fun.

In my prayer room, my Secret Place, I said, "Holy Spirit, I release them to a violent end. I will not pray for their salvation. I will pray for You to correct them. If You need to bring them to a violent end so that their network of evil people will wake up and cry out to God for mercy and forgiveness, I ask You to do so."

God used two people to shake up a nation. Ananias and Sapphira were allowed to fall dead in the church. The Bible says then there was great fear of the Lord, which is the beginning of Wisdom. The fear of God came upon the early church.

The point I want to make here is that God is interested in your blessing. In one place Jesus said, "If you being evil, love to give good gifts to your children, how much more does your Heavenly Father love to give gifts to you?" In another place He said He would love to give the gift of The Holy Spirit to you.

God looks for Receivers. God is a Giver. He said to Adam, "I want you to receive a garden from Me." Then He said, "I want you to receive a wife from Me."

Freely you have received. Freely give.

"Mike, what comes first, giving or receiving?"

Receiving. You cannot give until you have received. We always taught you have to give *before* you receive anything. *What do you have to give if you have not received something?*

God *starts* every relationship with *receiving.*

We receive breath.

We receive the help of a doctor.

We receive the womb of our mother.

We receive parents; our mother, father.

We even take in oxygen and put it out again.

There is a cycle, but you enter the world as a Receiver. Then He says, "Now that you have found out about receiving and what you have received, I want you to know how to enter into a relationship with Me and how to give."

When we know God has shown us mercy, we should sow that mercy to others. Luke 6:38, in the total focus of the context, says if you give mercy to people, you give forgiveness to people, you have authorization to receive.

Freely you have given, so you can freely receive.

When you are poor you feel *inferior.*

When you are poor you feel *ashamed.*

When you are poor you have *no influence.*

The Bible says one man had a lot of Wisdom in helping a city with strategy, but because he had no money, nobody listened to him. This is an unpleasant truth.

Poverty Can Diminish Your Influence. This is not true in every case. There are people all over the world who, even though they're poor, have affected the world. Their fasting and mobilization of other poor people brought change.

But there is something very powerful about a man who has the money to go on television and buy $5,000,000.00 worth of advertisement. He has influence.

Why are men poor?

2. Men Are Poor Because They Refuse To Be Taught. "*Poverty and shame cometh to him that* *refuseth instruction."*

3.   Men Are Often Poor Because They Have A Philosophy That God Created And Predestined Their Poverty.

4.   Men Are Poor Because They Resent The Wealthy And Refuse To Learn Anything From Them.

5.   Men Stay Poor Because They Refuse To Embrace The Opportunities Given To Them.

Twice I stopped for a man on the corner with a sign saying, *Will Work for Food.* I got out, gave him a $100.00 bill and said, "You just got a job. Get in the car." I did that 3 times in a row and never had one man get in the car. Not one.

They wanted my $100.00 bill. They wanted money. They wanted to be sponsored. Think about that.

Money Is A Tool.

A weaponless warrior has no power. Who fears a man without a gun or, you know, a soldier that has no gun? Nobody.

So a Christian without money almost feels weaponless.

Do I believe in prayer? Absolutely. Do I believe that prayer can do what money does? No.

A man told me, "I do everything by prayer."

I said, "Good, I am going to follow you to the airport. I want to see how you buy your ticket through prayer. I want to see you get a ticket without money."

My father prayed 4 to 10 hours a day. He built 7 churches.

I really believe in praying for blessing, for Prosperity, and praying for problems to be solved. I do not want to hurt your prayer life at all, but I do not pray for money.

▶ I pray about *how to show Honor.*
▶ I pray about *where to sow my Favor.*
▶ I pray about *where to sow my energy.*
▶ I pray about *how to solve a problem.*

Prosperity Is The Fruit of Solving A Problem. That is why I pray for direction.

I was born and raised in a Christian home, a Pentecostal pastor's home. My father is now in his late 90's. We never had, that I remember, two slices of bologna on the same sandwich.

I said to my father during a service a few years ago, "Daddy, do you remember any times during our time at home with 7 kids that we had two slices of bologna on the same sandwich?"

He said, "Never."

We had no money. My father's highest salary was $125.00 a week, and out of the $125.00 he fed, clothed and took care of 7 children, paid his own house note, his own car note, and bought his own gasoline. They did not have housing allowance in those days like we think of it. That is the most he ever made.

Before then he was making $92.50 in Central Gardens in Nederland, Texas when I was a teenage boy of 13 or 14 years old. He fed all of us. The meal I most recall from the time back at home is chicken gumbo. The gumbo was made with chicken necks. Not chicken breasts and thighs, *chicken necks.*

I learned to *hate* poverty. I *still* have a hatred of poverty, and I am a little different than most preachers. I am not going to tell you that you should *accept* it.

You Can Use Your Faith To Escape A Problem, or To Endure A Problem.

6. They Do Not Know The Philosophy or

The Character of God. They do not understand the character of God. God is not a stingy, mean rascal. God is a giving, loving Father. The Bible continuously speaks about God's desire that we receive from the Lord.

He said to Adam, "Receive this garden. Receive a wife."

In John 1:11 we learn of Jesus, "He came unto His own, but His own received Him not." A Jewish friend watches my television program. I just want to say from my heart; because you have met a so-called Christian does not mean that you have met somebody who really knows Jesus.

I believe with all of my heart that receiving Jesus is vital today. I want to present that truth before I go any further.

I understand that 50 percent of the wealth of the world may be in the hands of Jewish people. I understand many things about world finances. I know God had a covenant with Abraham that those who were of his blood would have an anointing, a grace upon them for the Prosperity of God.

Abraham entered into a covenant, not just with Melchizedek, but into a covenant with God. Then God said, "Everyone who blesses you will be blessed. Everyone who curses you will be cursed," (read Genesis 12:3).

I do not know that Washington, D.C., knows it, but in Christianity, in the United States, we're fully persuaded that our reaction to the Jewish nation of Israel, determines God's reaction to us. *The reaction of the United States to Israel will determine God's reaction to America.*

When America becomes *disloyal* to the nation of

Israel, America will be dismantled like a billion ants scattering on a loaf of bread. If America does not remain loyal to Israel, America will be dismantled, because a person or a nation's Future is in its alliances.

Lucifer *rebelled* against God in the Heavens but a third of the angels were kicked out because of their alliance with Lucifer. I believe there is a great understanding to be had about the power of who I am in alignment with.

Understanding the character of God is critically important. The character of God has to be explored.

- ▶ God said, "You can ask anything in My Name, and I will give it to you."
- ▶ God said, "The silver and the gold are Mine."
- ▶ God said, "I see the hairs on your head. I know the number."
- ▶ God said, "I even see the sparrow that falls from the tree, and if I care about the sparrow that I created, how much more do I care about you?"

Never forget that God was trying in The Word to show us, "I am concerned about you."

Let me share some personal feelings:

I care about you.

Your life matters to me.

Do you have what you *need?*

Do you have what you *want?*

Are you able to live a stress-free life?

When somebody does not have a car, I care. When somebody is homeless, I care. No, I cannot underwrite the whole world, but there must be a hatred of poverty. You must have an understanding of God.

7. Men Stay Poor If They Resent Prosperity. If they resent the wealthy, they will stay poor, because you can't learn from someone you resent.

8. Men Stay Poor Because They Have Never Investigated The Divine Deposits God Has Placed In Them. You can live a lifetime and never identify your gifts, your skills and your talents.

9. Men Stay Poor Because They Ignore The Opportunity To Learn, To Become Protégés. I have just about given up any private protégé teaching unless I am believed. If I tell you this is what you need to do and you do not do it, then you should stay broke. You should stay poor. I would not even want you to be blessed, because then you would have a perverted philosophy.

A lady that worked for me one time said, "I am homeless. I have nowhere to live."

I said, "Okay, I have a house and I am going to let you live in that house for 'X' amount of money. I think you ought to lease out one room for one-half the cost of the mortgage, that way you get the house half paid for. At the end of the year you will have an extra several thousand dollars."

She looked at the house and said, "I did not feel right in it."

This was somebody that did not have a house. This is someone that had no money. Yet she said, "Uh, I did not feel right."

I told one lady that lived in a house I owned, "I am going to knock off about $20,000.00 from the price. It is appraised for $20,000.00 more. It is good for your children, and your monthly payment can go to the amount of money you owe. I won't even charge you interest. You can just buy it. Everything is pure principal."

She said, "One of the faucets is broken."

I said, "It can be fixed."

I found out she was looking at $250,000.00 houses in another subdivision.

I asked, "Why are you looking at a $250,000.00 house?"

She said, "I have faith."

"Oh. Okay. If you have so much faith, you do not need me."

Why am I telling you this? Because I do not know that I have met one really poor person that would learn anything from me.

10. Men Stay Poor Because They Despise Correction.

11. Men Often Stay Poor Because They Consider Themselves A Victim of Life.

12. Some Men Stay Poor Because They Believe Their Nationality or Their Race Has Made Them Predestined For Poverty.

13. Some Men Stay Poor Because They Have Never Been Taught The Rewards of Money.

Someone says, "I have met some bad people that had money." I have met some bad people that are broke, too. I have met some bad people that drove a car. Should I quit driving a car? I have met bad people that ate at a restaurant. Should I stop eating at a restaurant because some bad people ate at a restaurant?"

"What are you trying to do, Mike?"

I am trying to provoke the fire out of you. I am trying to provoke you to hate poverty. There is no good thing in poverty. You can hardly help anybody when you are broke. You can't provide a safe house for your children.

I bought a house for a young man that traveled with me. A year later he still had not moved into that house, or even painted it.

I said, "Son, I bought you a house. Why are you waiting to move in?"

"There are some things I want to do, and I am going to. I have decided exactly how I want the house to be."

Think of living in a rent house for a whole year after I gave you a house.

I have had people get mad after I bought them a car, but I did not buy the insurance.

14. I Have Never Met Anybody Poor Who Stayed Poor If They Were Thankful. If a person is thankful, *they become a magnet.* They become a magnet for good events in their life.

Do you have any idea the *fragrance* of a thankful person? Have you ever been around somebody who is grateful? I do not mean, "Thank you. Thanks so much." I am not talking about that kind of gratitude where the individual makes an event out of it.

Have you ever been around someone who truly was grateful for what you just did and you felt it?

Gratitude is *not a two-word sentence.*

Gratitude *emanates from somebody's life.*

Gratitude is *a fragrance and an environment.*

You know when somebody's thankful, and you know when they're not. You know when somebody gets up from a table after you just coughed up $50.00 for them and they never say, "Thank you." Their 5 kids made the night miserable. When you have done all of that and they never really are thankful, sometimes bitterness comes.

There is nothing that will drive you crazier than to sponsor an unthankful human. Jesus had it right. 90 percent of humans are unthankful.

He gave us the percentage when, after He had healed the 10 lepers, only one returned to express His appreciation.

I know some would say, "I think they were so excited they could not believe it. They went to tell all their friends, and forgot to come back."

Jesus did not forget. Jesus did not look at that like that. He said, "I want to know where the 9 are. What happened to the unthankful?"

I bought a car for a person one time, and their reaction was, "It is about time I get a Harvest. I have sowed so much. It is about time God answered my prayer."

I said, "He answered your prayer my eye. God had nothing to do with this. He has had 15 years to buy you a car, and it never happened until I walked in. God did not buy this car. I bought this car."

An unthankful person is a person who minimizes the human God worked through. They trivialize because they do not want the responsibility of having to be thankful.

Think on this. Think on this truth about gratitude. Why would a billionaire worth $20,000,000,000.00 leave nothing to his children and everything to a zoo?

Why does a guy worth $100,000,000.00 with 3 children leave nothing to his children but $1.00 each, and leave everything to his nurse? He had unthankful children. His unthankful children had 40 years to prove they were grateful to a father who fed them, preserved them, and watched over them. Think about that.

15. Some Men Stay Poor Because They Never Celebrate The Givers In Their Life. They stay broke because they think everybody *owes* them something.

16. People Stay Poor Because They are Unthankful For The Opportunities To Work. They consider work torturous. They come in 15 minutes late and want to sit by the time clock 30 minutes before it's time. They have off Saturday, and if you call them in, they will be too busy.

Who are the top 5 people who will pay you to do a job right now? Give me 5 telephone numbers you call, and say, "I am available," and be hired. Name me 5 people who would pay you for any given day.

You are 40 years old. You are 50 years old. Tell me 5 people you can call who will say, "Come right on over. I will write you a check today."

I have 3 names on my desk. I am keeping these names. These 3 people come up to me after church and said, "I would like to be a problem-solver in your life."

Not one of them said, "Give me some money and I will solve your problems." They just said, "I would like to solve your problems. I can hardly wait to go get my list of problems."

Money is no mystery. Do not try to be a genius. Look for a problem close to you.

Every Problem Close To You Is An Invitation To A Relationship.

Everywhere There Is A Problem There Is A Future.

A Problem Is An Invitation To Build Credibility.

A Problem Is An Invitation To Prove Your Competence.

A Problem Is An Invitation To Reveal Your Difference From Everybody Else.

What is your reaction to a problem?

A few years ago, I called one of my tech people to

my house. He is not on staff now, but then I said, "I cannot figure out this phone. I am about to go to Nigeria, and I need it to be set for overseas. They said, "There is a way to set it."

I came in late that night, at 10:30, and walked into my office. The phone was there with a note from a man who was full-time on my staff, "I could not figure it out."

I hop on the plane and I fly to New York. I get off the plane. One of my protégés is there and I said, "Son, after I speak tonight I have to fly to another place, but I will be back Tomorrow night. I want you to take my phone to Verizon and have them fix this where I can go overseas."

I flew back the next day. He meets me at the airport. He is happy. He is wonderful. He is a nice kid, wonderful, loves God, and loves me. I said, "Did you take the phone to Verizon and get it fixed?"

He said, "I could not figure that out, Dr. Murdock. I spent two hours on that phone and I could not figure it out." He handed it back to me.

I said, "I did not ask you to figure it out. I told you to take it to Verizon."

"Yeah, I could not figure it out."

I said, "But I did not ask you. I asked you to take it to Verizon." Stupid has an odor, and it can leave you sick for hours.

I went to Chicago. A young pastor on the staff of Dr. Robb Thompson's church, *Family Harvest*, met me at the airport. I looked at him and I said, "You're the third person I am asking for help with this. I can't figure out the code on how to get this ready for overseas."

He said, "I will have it ready, Dr. Murdock, by 10:00 Tomorrow morning."

When I walked in the church he handed me the phone and said, "Here is the laminated card of the steps it takes to get that. It is ready to go right now. And when you get through today, there will be another phone that never requires you to do any setting changes so you will have two phones for your trip to Nigeria. I bought you another phone as a gift so you will never have to worry about this phone again."

That is excellence. I do not want non-excellent people in my world. I want people who solve problems. I want people who watch me drink warm tea, and say, "I think he is ready for another one." That is the kind of folks I want in my life.

I want someone to notice I hadn't eaten all day. If I get through preaching at a church for two hours and its 10:30 at night, I would like somebody in my circle to notice I need food and drink...sustenance.

I do not want someone to say to me, "Would you like some water?"

Then I can say back, "Oh no, I am a camel. I can go 9 days."

"Want anything to eat?"

"No, I am fasting. This is my 49th day."

I want a problem-solver. Are you a problem-solver? If you aren't there is no reason for you to be in anybody else's life.

17. Men Stay Poor Because They Never Look At The Problem At Hand. They ignore the needs of others.

Our church sometimes feeds 1,000 families every week. These are people who are out of jobs, going through difficult places. I needed some work done at my house and I called one of my pastors, "Pastor, I need somebody to move some furniture for me, and to do some basic things at my house. Can you get me 4 people who are out of jobs? I will pay them legitimate wages to come help me today because I have so much at my house to do."

He called back and said, "I can't find anybody to work for you."

I said in my Mind, "I am feeding 1,000 families every week who are out of jobs and cannot buy food. I open the house and ask, "Would you come to my house and help me do some work today?" I could not find one who would come. That is all across America.

The Bible says, "Poverty and shame shall be to him that refuseth instruction," (Proverbs 13:18).

I hate poverty. I despise it and I do not think it's necessary.

"Brother Mike, you sound harsh."

I am. I hate poverty and there are people in countries making $2.00 a day, and here in America we can make $100.00 a day. We can open our eyes and make $100.00 a day. God has been good to us. God has been merciful to us.

I do not care how many times we gripe and we complain. You do not owe your Harvest to a human.

What God has given you in reward for your work, your time, your toil, and your labor is *yours.* When you sow, whether it's to the poor or to help somebody going through a problem, you have every right to *expect* the blessing of the Lord to rest upon your life.

How do you react when somebody has a problem? How do you react when your boss has a problem?

Paul wrote to the church at Thessalonica and said, "If you do not work, you do not eat."

He made everything so plain. He said, "Don't even have a meal with somebody who refuses to work. Have no company with him."

He also said, "Don't hate them. Love them like a brother, but do not lend credibility to somebody who refuses to work."

Did you know Wal-Mart gets sued every two hours?

Somebody's hamburger did not have onions, or somebody did not look and there was a hole in the ground, so they sue McDonald's.

Wal-Mart has been the number one employer in the world for a while. Apple is probably the top company for excellence, but Wal-Mart has hired thousands of families, and yet people will picket Wal-Mart. They will do everything to bring them down.

People do not have a respect for opportunity.

There are a lot of *cheap* people in Christianity. Restaurant owners have told me that Christians on Sunday are the cheapest, stingiest people they deal with. They'll eat a big meal and never leave the server anything but some ridiculous tract that looks like money. You turn them over and it says, "Fooled you, didn't I? You thought this was money. Satan will fool you, too." Have you ever seen those? Stupid!

☙ 4 ❧

QUESTIONS HOST ANSWERS ON THE EARTH

Questions..."Create" Your Answers.

I trust this Question and Answer session from *Why Do Men Stay Poor?* will open 1,000 doors for you.

Guest #1 Question. How can I know when I am in the wrong geographical area?

Dr. Mike Murdock: That is a good question. How do you think you can know? What are your thoughts so far?

Guest: During the previous 30 years of my life, I was successful in an area, and blessing was reaching me without reaching for it. Now I am in another state area, and everything is dead.

Dr. Mike Murdock: Two illustrations in the Bible come to my Mind.

Obviously the first is 1 Kings 17. When the brook dried up, God did not ask Elijah to command the brook to produce. Elijah received a *second* command.

I consider a dried up brook to be an instruction. The second illustration is from when the wells were stolen and taken away from Isaac. Every time he tried something else, they stole that one. I think Isaac dug 3 wells before he finally got what was his.

He did not battle. He did not fight over it. He recognized that the God who gave him the first was the supplier of the second. *We always reap where we sow.* I have not. I have sown a lot in one area and gone down the road and had God bless me in another zone, in another territory.

I feel like there are things that confirm the direction of God in my life.

1. Is There Opportunity In My Environment? Is there opportunity for my gift? You probably heard me talk about David. God never told David to fight Goliath. David saw opportunity to use his gift.

2. Is There Favor? Are you in the field of Favor? Naomi told Ruth, "Stay in this rich man's view. He needs to see you. Stay where he can see you. This man likes you." The rich man, Boaz, said, "Leave handfuls on purpose for her."

What I would do is begin to prepare for leaving Egypt. I would prepare for Canaan. I would identify where there is Favor. I believe Favor talks.

I do not want to be where I am not celebrated. I have no business there. It has nothing to do with need. There may be people in your environment that desperately need you.

Paul wrote to Titus, "I am going to send you to Crete. The Cretans are known to be soulless people who are ruled by their bellies." Paul made some negative statements.

He said, "These people are little rats."

"For that cause, I am sending you there to set things in order."

Unless God has given you a direct command, stay

there to set things in order.

I think I would begin to look for where there is Favor. Favor is a two-way street. It does not mean that every time somebody opens the door, you walk in. *No.*

Do you have Favor toward that person? In my life, I have often responded to someone who needed my Favor, but did not show me Favor.

Leave them. Do not do it. Do not invest where there is not Favor.

I have been at this church for a number of years. These people never have come one time to hear me preach on a Sunday morning. I have business people here in Fort Worth that come to my church about once a year and send me notes, "I want to do business with you."

I am here every Sunday morning and Wednesday night preaching my little heart out, and you do not have enough sense to drive 10 minutes to hear me preach? You're not going to do business with me.

You want my Favor, but you do not give me any Favor. No. I go where people are willing to invest in me.

Everybody will need your investment. There is nobody who will turn down a $100.00 bill. Nobody.

The Antichrist will take your money.

I only go where they show me Favor, and where I feel Favor toward them.

Guest #2 Question: How will I know that I am qualified for my Assignment?

Dr. Mike Murdock: That is a good question. You do know you have to be qualified.

Let me tell you some qualifications I think a

person has to have for an Assignment.

Do they create ease or disease? Do they create comfort or discomfort when they enter an environment?

I am thinking of Abigail. Her servants trusted her so much they shared the secret of David's rejection by her husband, Nabal, with her. She could be trusted with private information. She was capable.

Boaz said, "All of my servants speak well of you. People that I trust speak well of you." Ruth created credibility with those that Boaz trusted.

Ask yourself, "Do I increase credibility? What did I do today to increase my credibility?"

Ruth saw the necessity of increasing her credibility. She was faithful. She was consistent.

For Ruth to qualify for Boaz, it wasn't the kinship. He really wasn't her closest kin. He had Biblical right to deny her, but he told her, "Others are discussing you, and they're telling me that you treat Naomi better than 7 sons would treat their mother."

First, You Have To Become. If you are ready for your Assignment, you would be there. If you are ready for your Future, you would be there.

Abigail knew what David wanted.

Abigail was discreet with her husband, Nabal, who was a rich fool. God killed him 10 days after he disrespected David.

Inside every man lives both a king and fool. The one you address is the one who will respond. Abigail later married David because he was so impressed that she talked to the king in him instead of the fool.

Abigail did not try to correct or train David.

Ruth did not try to control nor train Boaz.

Esther did not tell the king, "I do not care if you

plan for me to bathe and soak in oil for 12 months, I am the most beautiful woman here and I have a say so."

Abigail kept trouble down by solving a problem caused by her husband's mistakes. She went to David and gave him the food he wanted. She did not say, "Why do not you fast? You're crazy."

Phoebe was commended by the Apostle Paul. The Apostle Paul was a cranky Holy Ghost man who had an opinion about everybody and everything. God anointed him and used him. Paul said, "I commend unto you Phoebe."

He actually presented to the church someone who had been a blessing. My father used Phoebe as an example of my mother.

Leadership Should Know Your Qualifications. People in authority should be the ones to approve of you. They should know you well enough to say you are ready for your Assignment.

A woman said to me, "I want you to ordain me at The Wisdom Center."

I wrote her back and said, "I do not know you. I am not going to give you credibility that you have not earned. I am not going to tell everybody that you are all right. I do not even know you. I have not heard you preach. I have not heard you do anything."

She got mad, which was proof right there.

Esther did not correct the king. Esther did not even tell him, "Aren't you an idiot for letting Haman be your best friend? What kind of king are you?"

Ruth, reacted properly when Boaz said, "You're not my closest kin. I do not know if I want you or not. I will see if this other guy wants you."

Ruth did not say, "You do not know what you have

here. You have no idea what you have just lost."

You Are Ready For Your Assignment When You Know Whose Advice Matters. You demonstrate readiness by the advice you are willing to pursue.

A young man working for me said, "I have made this decision."

When he finished telling me everything he was going to do, I said, "I want you to remember that you have never asked me for my counsel, so you will not receive it. You have made a decision without my counsel, so do not ever tell anybody you are my protégé. You have not even asked for me to pray. You have not even informed me ahead of time."

The young man replied, "I want to leave with your blessing."

I said, "I cannot bless you. I can pray for you, but I can't bless you. I only bless somebody that is doing what I believe is in the will of God. I am not going to pray for God to bless you, when I do not know that you are in the will of God. I have to pray with faith."

I Believe You Know That You Are Ready For Your Assignment When The People That Are Involved With You Show You Favor. How did Joseph know he was ready for the palace? When Pharaoh *invited* him.

How do you know you are ready for marriage? If the guy asks you.

You want to look wherever you are Assigned.

I had a good person, a person close to my heart, say to me, "God has told me I am your next personal assistant."

I said, "That is not even His decision. It is mine. Go back and talk to the God. My assistant is my decision. That is not God's decision. It is mine."

Look wherever you believe you are assigned. If you believe you are assigned to a bank but the manager says, "No, we are not hiring." You can go back 20 times, but you want to be prepared.

Your environment needs to be ready for you, and you need to be ready for your environment. I have hired people because I liked them, but they were not prepared for this environment.

I think this is the wisest question you could ask right now. You'll know when the Assignment door is open. *When a door opens, you know you are ready.* The door stays closed until you are ready.

It was Pharaoh that needed to be ready. Joseph had to be ready, too.

Guest #3 Question: You said a friend of yours, a preacher, said if someone's finances are running down, especially if they had money before, it means there is somebody within the circle that is out of the will of God.

Dr. Mike Murdock: Yes, that was David Wilkerson, author of one of the best-selling books of all-time, *The Cross and The Switchblade.*

I am trying to think of a Scriptural reason that God would make it hard for you to leave so that you would stay there in His will, or His timing.

I do not know that God withheld any money. Certainly God could, but I do not think God keeps you poor, so you will be humble, or keeps you poor so you will intercede.

There is a Law of Sowing and Reaping. God works with my faith.

I think a lot of people feel like robots. They ask, "Lord, where do You want me to go? Lord, what do You want me to do?"

There is a place in God where faith rises. It becomes like when the rain was withheld because Elijah had said, "It shall not rain."

There is a place in God where I believe that God honors your decisions. If you say, "God, this is the way I am going. This is what I want to do," God will allow you to go your own way.

One night I was at a church service, and I was about to receive an Offering. I was trying to be real spiritual and I asked, "God, what is it You want? What do You want me to believe You for? What's here tonight for my ministry?"

It was like the Lord looked at me with disgust. The Holy Spirit said, "It is your ministry. What do you want to happen?"

There is a fascinating Scripture that a lot of people misunderstand, but I really believe it. The Lord said, "Command ye Me, the work of My hands."

"You tell me." Here's the reason I say that. Do you remember where the Bible said Jesus could not do many works because of the unbelief in that city? That is why He left Nazareth and went to Capernaum? He could not do many works.

If doubt can stop God's hands, then faith can unlock God's hands. There are times that God just says, "What do you want?" Then you speak it.

"Death and life are the power of the tongue," (Proverbs 18:21). If you are going through a destitute place where it seems like nothing is right, I would take action.

My mother taught me and I believed her, "If you do not know the will of God, assume a direction and tell

God to stop it if it is not right."

My mother said, "If I do not know what direction to go and what God wants from my life, I assume a direction."

Mother continued, "I say, 'Lord, I cannot seem to hear what You want, so I am going this direction, because I believe this is the right direction, and if it is not, You stop it.'"

This has really been a powerful principle that has been operating in my life for a long time.

Guest #4 Question: Dr. Mike, could God reveal something to somebody concerning an issue, and then not reveal it to the other person who is involved in that situation?

Dr. Mike Murdock: He did to Samuel with Eli. "Tell me, what did God tell you?" Eli asked Samuel. Then Samuel said, "Because you did not keep your sons pure before The House of the Lord, God is going to take away your power."

God did tell Samuel something He did not tell Eli, and yet it concerned Eli.

Nathan, the prophet, went to David, and told the king what was going to happen to him. Sometimes it's up to a prophet just to tell that person what the Lord has spoken. So, yes, it's possible. It is possible God will tell one person, and not tell the other.

I am reluctant in that area because I have had people come to me and say, "God told me I was going to marry you."

I then say, "He has not told me."

I thought I was going to marry somebody one time, but it was not the Lord. So I am asking the Lord to confirm things. It is good for God to confirm things to you. I would pray, "Lord, if this is Your will, reveal this to them."

Guest #5 Question: My question is for those of us protégés that are in the ministry. It is simply this, How do we sustain our ministry when the streams of financial Favor dry up?

Dr. Mike Murdock: That is a good question. I will tell you how the Lord's dealt with me.

Dr. Lester Sumrall said something so strong to me. I am going to share with you in light of the whole spectrum. He told me one day, "If a man cannot raise his own support, he is not called."

Do you see how strong that is?

"If a man cannot raise his own support, he is not called."

When I thought about that I wondered, "What does that mean?" *A man needs to learn how to raise his own support.*

I have had streams to dry up in my ministry when I was working my head off. I mean, I worked my head off and I was still going straight down. A man took over my TV time and I did not realize it for like 12 weeks.

I had bills pile up, and I had gone off the air. I had no support. I will tell you how the Lord dealt with me. I believe God uses dried up finances to drive you away from the brook.

In 1 Kings 17, we learn there is a Divine message in lack. If the brook dries up, there is a new instruction I need to receive from the Lord.

This is a little delicate, but it must be addressed. I feel like when the finances dry up, there are

Biblical reasons for it drying up.

One of the reasons is there can be a widow in Zarephath who must be challenged. If Elijah's brook did not dry up, Elijah would have never gone to Zarephath.

Why did God have to dry up the brook and cause the raven to stop showing up? Then God said, "Now, it is time for you to go to Zarephath."

A dried up brook in the ministry is a Divine command telling you somebody under your ministry is struggling financially. *Unlock their faith.* God lets the Deliverer feel the pain of the Captive.

If a ministry has plenty, generally speaking, if they say nothing and do nothing, they let the people's giving stay the same. But when a ministry starts having a difficulty, many think, "I have a problem. I better get the people to support me." It is really the opposite. *The ministry is having a problem because the people are having a problem.* God lets you feel their problem so that you can unlock their faith.

God had fed Elijah miraculously. Elijah did not *need* the widow. God had fed Elijah *without* a partner. Can God feed a ministry without partners? Every day of His life.

It is the partner who needs the minister. Until the partner sows into the ministry, the partner has no Future. The Lord has dealt with me on this.

You are in the pulpit doing the work of a Bishop. You are trying to make ends meet, but you know there is no meat in the storehouse. Malachi 3 says, "That there may be meat in My house." You know there is no meat in the church. There is no meat in the House of God.

Why? Somebody's not tithing. He said, "Bring the Tithe and give Offerings so there will be meat in My house." So, if there is no meat in the House of the Lord, somebody is not doing their part.

Why is someone not tithing? Why is someone not sowing? *Their faith has not been provoked. Their partnership has not been birthed.* I believe that lack in the ministry, is a God-command telling you, "Go out and unlock the Seeds of the people."

A famous preacher asked me to come help him that I was watching on TV. I was mad at the preacher. Something had gone wrong, and I was upset with him on a personal thing.

I saw him struggling. He was really, really, really struggling, so I made a statement out loud to the Lord. I said, "If he calls me in the next two days, I will go help him."

I received two phone calls two days in a row. "Please come help," he said.

I was with Brother Oral Roberts the day before, and I said, "Brother Roberts, there is a preacher who wants me to help him raise funds and support for a hotel." I said, "I do not feel like raising support for a hotel."

Brother Oral Roberts looked at me and said in a condescending way, "Oh, Mike, you are not raising money for a hotel. You are unlocking the Seeds of the people, and they need the Harvest."

If, in the ministry, we had plenty in every account, the day would come we would not even pass an Offering, and what would happen? *The people would go broke.*

If partners do not hear, and God has to let the

brook dry up to make a preacher get off of his rear end and walk away from the meal the raven has brought, the pressure causes him to unlock the Seeds of the people.

God has blessed me in other ways, and so I do not touch a penny of the Tithe and Offerings of The Wisdom Center, but I actually have been convicted by The Holy Spirit for how I have handled things.

At times I have felt that God is going to do something different, because the people here at The Wisdom Center need to support a preacher. They need to *support* a man of God, but sometimes there is a pride in us.

"I do not need your Tithe. God's blessed me in other ways, and I do not need your Tithe." There is a form of pride in that.

The Bible says in Ezekiel that God has made it, as you know, where we are to sow up. *Every Seed Has A Different Future.* What your people give to the church is a totally different Seed than what they will sow and give into you.

It is a total different Harvest. Twice a year, during Mentor's Month in October, and on my birthday in April; twice a year, we allow people to sow a Seed into my life.

I give to preachers, not just to churches. I sow in ministers, because I want their anointing to flow. A Seed is a *conduit.* A Seed is a *channel.* When I sow into a man of God, everything in that man of God, as Paul said, "We become partakers of the grace that is in him."

When I started giving to my daddy, not just to his organization, I *gave* to my father, that anointing began to *grow* in me. *It is imperative for the people to be linked to a personal anointing.*

A preacher can do other things to make money. You can go sell cars. You can sell insurance. You can make money at a thousand different things, but God wants the people to have a link to that anointing.

People have to be taught to sow into a minister.

I felt embarrassed when Dr. Mike Brown was receiving an Offering of Honor for me. He said, "I want Dr. Murdock to come sit in this chair. I want us to lay the Offering at his feet."

I felt like a dog. I felt like I have to tell him, "Don't ever do this again." I was so embarrassed. I was sitting in the chair on the platform, and some of the people, instead of just laying the Offering there for me, some of them would kneel down and pray for me or touch my feet.

I thought, "Lord, I will be struck dead here." I wanted to say, "I am a man, just like you are. Get up." But there is something supernatural about *blessing* a man of God.

Several years ago I was in a service with Bishop Jerry Grillo. The Lord told me to wash he and his wife's feet. I could not stop crying, and my Mind was going crazy. I was embarrassed. I did not want people to think I was doing it for a show.

If I were going to do a show, it would not be washing people's feet. But I was washing his feet and I was crying and crying and crying. My crying was over, "How beautiful are the feet of them that carry the Gospel, that carry the good news."

I thought of when the woman washed the feet of Jesus with the perfume and broke the alabaster box. She was wiping His feet. Do you remember when Jesus washed His disciples' feet?

Who would ever imagine Jesus washing Judas' feet, or Peter's, or John's? Imagine Jesus washing their feet, but there is transference.

I was in a church where a pastor had on his Tithe envelope a place where they could bless their pastor. The line read, "I want to sow this Seed for my pastor's teaching."

Something leaped in my heart. Hardly any preacher will do that because of critical people.

A few weeks ago, it happened here at The Wisdom Center. The Lord dealt with me about it. The Offering wasn't large, about $3,000.00, but the church gave me a Christmas Seed. They received an opportunity to sow into my life.

The fact is they need that. They need it. Stress The Tithe. Today I felt a grace come on me to pray for new tithers. We had several come forward, and something unlocked inside me.

We're talking about covenant with God's work. If a building of brick and stones that focuses on The Word of God are important, how much more important is flesh and blood?

Do it for 90 days, and then get them to write in the back of their Bible the day that they did it. Watch the Miracles that happen for them.

❧ 5 ❧

PROSPERITY IS THE REWARD OF OBEDIENCE

⬛▶◉◀⬛

Great Preachers Always Have A Theme.

Proverbs 4:7 tell us, "Wisdom is the principal thing." This Scripture establishes my focus and my chosen priority.

Oral Roberts told me once the greatest mistake pastors ever make is *preaching a new sermon every service.* He said if you listen to any man of God, he'll have a theme for his life, and at the most God only gives a man one or two themes or a focus for his life, at the most.

I have watched the wonderful evangelist Billy Graham establish as his theme, Jesus died on The Cross, rose again, and He is coming back to earth and He will heal your brokenness, He will heal your confusion.

My obsession is Wisdom.

Some weeks ago, a man tried to act like he was very disinterested in Prosperity. I said, "Make me a list of everything you can accomplish without money, then I will show you my list of everything that you can accomplish with money."

Proverbs 4:5, "Get Wisdom…" You are born with instincts, *not Wisdom.* "Get Wisdom, get understanding, forget it not. Neither decline from the words of My mouth. Forsake her not and she shall preserve thee."

God Did Not Take Responsibility For Preserving You. He Assigned The Responsibility of Taking Care of Ourselves.

A man accused me of not trusting The Lord because I locked my car doors.

I said, "Well, it's not the Lord I am distrusting. I never had a fear He'd break in."

Proverbs 4:7, "Wisdom is the principal thing."

What is Wisdom?

Wisdom Is The Ability To Anticipate The Consequence.

Wisdom Is A Scriptural Reaction To An Earthly Problem.

Wisdom Is The Ability To Recognize Difference.

Difference in an *environment.*

Difference in a *moment.*

Difference in *countenance.*

Difference in *value.*

My hair is important, but my fingers are more important. My fingers are important, but not as important as my eyes. My eyes are important, but not as important as my heart and my blood system.

Wisdom Is The Ability To Identify True Value.

Proverbs 2:12, 16 reference recognizing someone's difference...who is evil...identifying false voices in your environment.

"Wisdom is the principal thing. Therefore, get Wisdom and with all thy getting get understanding. Exalt her and she shall promote thee. She shall bring thee to Honor," (Proverbs 4:7-8).

Circle the word "Honor" in your Bible. *Honor Is*

The Rewarding of Someone For Their Difference.

You may be showing Honor to the elderly.

You may be showing Honor to a great achiever.

One of the wealthiest men I ever knew with $12,000,000.00 gave his 5 best friends a new Rolls Royce each Christmas. *I laughingly said I was friend number 6.*

He told me, "Never be in an environment without recognizing or honoring Greatness."

I asked, "What do you mean?" I was in my 30's. We were at lunch.

He said, "If somebody across the restaurant has been a remarkable and unusual achiever, write him a note, pick up his tab, pay his bill. Never be in the presence of Greatness without giving deference, without Offering recognition or Honor."

If I could have chosen my nationality I would be Filipino. The reason for that is the aura of Honor that is in Manila.

The airport security men who were checking our briefcases, our bags, were the most gracious men. It looked like they had been trained by the best of the best. There was not a rude tone. There was not a rude voice. They were so gracious. It was almost like I had given them a gift by letting them look in my briefcase. Something went through me.

I Want To Learn Honor. Honor has a Fragrance. Honor dispels coarseness and rudeness. Because of their beautiful sense of Honor, I have great admiration for that particular nationality of people.

Verse 8 says God will bring you to Honor through the Wisdom of God.

"Praise ye the Lord. Blessed is the man that

feareth the Lord, that delighteth greatly in His commandments. His Seed shall be mighty upon the earth:
the generation of the upright shall be blessed. Wealth
and riches shall be in his house: and his righteousness
endureth for ever," (Psalm 112:1-3).

There is a difference between The Person of Jesus
and The Principles He taught. The Gospel has two
parts. God loving you doesn't add a penny to your
checkbook. Loving God does not double your salary.
Just like your ear doesn't see and your eye doesn't
listen, every part has a specific function.

Every Law of God Creates A Different Fruit.

If I go north I have a different experience than if I
go south. If I take a ship I have a different experience
than if I take an airplane.

*Everything Is A Different Experience With A
Different Fruit.*

Every Person Is A Different Experience.

*Every Law Is Connected To A Different Reward
System.*

*The Person of Jesus Makes You Compatible With
Eternity.* He prepares you for eternity.

The Principles of Jesus Prepare You For The Earth.
The Person of Jesus creates your peace. The Laws of
God create your Prosperity.

It explains why a missionary can be broke, but he
has given his whole life to Christ. Alternately, you can
have a 22-year-old millionaire in New York that created
a new invention and he is worth $500,000,000.00.

Jesus said He would reward every man according
to his work.

Look at Proverbs 13:18. "Poverty and shame shall
be to him that refuseth instruction." Solomon was a

brilliant, intellectual man. He is conscious of God, conscious of The Laws of the earth, and he is describing a system of consequence.

We Live In A World of Rewards And Consequences.

When I was a young preacher I taught on *The Law of Inevitable Eventuality.* Everything is only an eventuality.

God never rewards you the day you obey Him because He gives you a season of waiting to document your trust. He never punishes you the day you sin, but He brings in a reward system of mercy. You could sin today and it may be 10 years before the consequence emerges, because *God gives you a season to turn around and make a change.* The character of God is impeccable. The character of God cannot be disputed.

Again, "Poverty and shame will be to him that refuseth instruction." But, now He is going to introduce you to a different world. *He is saying you can make a decision.*

There are 7 decisions that decide wealth.

"But he that regardeth a treasure, or receives or accepts reproof or correction shall be honored." Is that true?

Jeremiah 32:19, "Great in counsel, and mighty in work." The Holy Spirit is The Worker of The Godhead. He is the Producer. "For Thine eyes are open upon all the ways of the sons of men: to give," (Jeremiah 32:19).

God is in search of a Receiver. God is *passionate* about finding a Receiver. The whole Bible is a book about receiving. You must embrace that.

Just as excited as you are about receiving, there is ecstasy in the heart of God when He finds somebody qualified to receive.

Giving is the nature of God.
Giving is not a reaction of God.
Giving is the nature of God.

If God was reacting, most of us would have never received anything.

That is why receiving always comes before giving. Always. You have to receive before you can give. If you have never received anything, it's ludicrous to think that you have the ability to give. You enter the world receiving as a child.

You *receive* attention.
You *receive* affection.
You *receive* medical care.
You *receive* food from your mother.
You enter the world as a Receiver.

If you get good at it, there is no end to the reproductive Harvest systems of God. God said, "What you receive from Me can be measured, released, or multiplied by your ways."

Prosperity is *fruit.*
Prosperity is a *reward.*
Prosperity is an *incentive.*

Prosperity is offered as an incentive to believe in something God said.

1. Prosperity Is Having Enough Provision To Complete Divine Instructions. Prosperity is having enough money, energy, Favor and open doors to complete the Divine instruction.

2. Success Is The Obtaining of A Worthwhile Goal.

3. Wisdom Is The Ability To Recognize Difference In My World.

4. The Role of Wisdom Is To Identify Who

You Should Honor. The difference in poverty and Prosperity is simply who you have chosen to Honor. You cannot change your life until you change the voice you trust.

5.   Honor Is The Willingness To Reward Someone For Their Difference From You.

6.   Business Is Solving A Problem For A Monetary Reward.

"I have a problem. I need a hole dug over here."

"All right, give me $30.00, and I will dig the hole."

He digs the hole, he gets $30.00.

"I need some brick around this hole."

"That will be another $50.00."

Business is solving somebody's problem in exchange for some money. Business is taking your Mind, your hands, your energy, your knowledge and trading that for money. You are trading what you have, the Divine deposits within you.

Years ago I was in a little church in Washington, D.C. It was such a small place. I told the pastor, "Brother, I think you are making a mistake putting everything here. I have been coming to you now for about 5 years, and I do not think this is the place for your Seed."

He started talking to me and I said, "You could sell your knowledge. Call NBC. You know enough to sell your knowledge." Within about 90 days, he did. They gave him $250,000.00 per year for 3 days a week.

Forty-five years ago a famous preacher would fly up to New York for two days a week where he would sell his ideas to that bank. After those two days a week he would fly back to his church. You would know his name if I called it. They paid him $50,000.00 every month for those two days.

Something You've Been Given Has Monetary Value. Identify It.

Did you know that some people make $90.00 an hour for nodding and grunting the phrase, "And then how did you feel? Uh-huh. And then how did you feel? Uh-huh. And then how did you feel?"

Did you know a good listener makes more money than a guy who lays brick for hours?

Howard Hughes paid a man $500,000.00 a year when I was 18 years old just to put papers under the door, because he wanted nobody to know where he lived. Howard Hughes owned a hotel and he lived on the top floor. He was a recluse and wanted nobody to find him. He found one man that would not talk, and he gave that man $500,000.00 to slide business papers under the door.

You ask, "$500,000.00 a year for not talking?"

Try to find that gift. I will give you 5 or 6 years to try to find that kind of gift.

Have you identified the Divine deposits in you? Do you know what God has given you?

One of the major mistakes I made was when I released a disorganized young girl named Tammy. She was so disorganized that I finally let her go when I discovered *The Imperials* had tried to make an album of all my songs. She had been talking to them for two years. She had letters. They were begging for my songs, but she was so disorganized that the moment was lost.

I got so upset. I said, "Sit down. I am going to send you to Bible School." I paid her way to Rhema Bible College.

Two weeks later the office felt like we had had a death there. I could not figure out what was wrong. Something had really changed.

I had no idea my staff was so boring without her there. She was the catalyst for the energy in that environment. Nobody had life. I did not want anybody there. I had no idea that Tammy was the birther of all the energy and the excitement. She was constantly happy, always up. You could talk about the devil and she'd say, "He is persistent, isn't he?"

She saw nothing evil anywhere. I missed that because I see devils sitting under angel wings. One of the biggest mistakes I ever made in my lifetime was not identifying her uniqueness and realizing I needed her in my equation.

You Are The Missing Part In Somebody's Success Equation.

Have you inventoried what God has stored in you?

Neutralize Your Weakness By Magnifying The Divine Gift God Has Stored Inside You.

"Brother Mike, there is so much I do not know."

It is what you do know that God's going to bless. I do not get mad at McDonald's because they will not sell me a recliner. I am not there for a sofa. Identify what God has stored in you.

Focus must become important for you. Focus on your Prosperity. God is your Partner. Focus on Him. It is not an accident.

▶ Focus. When you wake up in the morning pray, "Father, thank You for my health, and my energy."

▶ Energy is currency; your hours are currency; your smile is currency.

▶ Your willingness to listen is currency. You're a walking gold mine. Have you found what's keeping God excited about you? Make it your focus.

▶ What are your skills? Inventory them.

▶ What is your level of passion for learning? You must become a professional learner. You must learn as a hobby. Become a habitual learner.

▶ Assess every environment you enter before you attempt to change, alter, correct, or control it.

In every environment, there is a leader, natural or self-appointed. *Identify the leader in each environment* and ask yourself, "What is my role in this environment? Am I the learner, or am I the teacher? Am I the mentor, or am I the listener? Something in me is needed or I would not be here."

I labor over my reactions. I went through the Pittsburgh Airport a few nights ago. They said I moved when I was standing in the scanner.

I was told, "He needs to search you." I do not think I ever made anybody as happy in my life as I made him. He began to fondle, and fondle, and fondle. If it wasn't public, they would have put him in prison for 20 years. I never got so angry in my life.

I thought, "Man, in 13 years of marriage I do not remember being loved this well." I was angry. I was agitated. I wanted to go back and create a scene.

Did I? No. I had to remind myself what I know.

Somebody asked me, "Do you live all of your Wisdom Keys?"

I said, "Not at the same time."

Something rolled in me. I wanted to throw it off,

but something inside me remembered reactions.

▶ Your reactions will decide *your successes.*

▶ Your reactions will decide *your failures.*

▶ Your reactions will decide *the Future of your marriage.*

▶ Your reactions decide *all of your progress and the Prosperity in your life.*

Lift your right hand high and say, "In The Name of Jesus, I am a Receiver of the Prosperity of God. I am a Receiver of Divine Wisdom. My reactions shall be appropriate and focused. I have great expectations of what God has put in me."

Business Is Solving A Problem For Monetary Reward. That is all business is, solving a problem. Do you remember when you were a little kid and you made lemonade and sold it in your front yard? I remember.

Do you remember putting ice in it, so your lemonade would go further?

Do you remember Offering it for 10 cents? I do. That is business.

God is into business. He wants to do business through you. See God doing business through you.

Who has a problem you can solve?

What have you been given to exchange?

What do you know that somebody else needs to know?

Until somebody has a problem, you do not have a Future. If somebody did not have a problem, there would be no marriages. There would be no salaries.

Problems Are Invitations To Reveal Your Competence.

Problems Are Invitations To A Reward System.

Joblessness is ludicrous. As long as there is a

problem on the earth, there is a job.

Everywhere There Is A Problem, There Is A Reward.

▶ A problem is a Seed for Divine multiplication.

▶ Everywhere there is a problem, there is the potential for you to reveal your difference from others.

▶ When you solve a problem, you show Honor, and everywhere you show Honor, you birth Favor.

▶ Everywhere there is Favor, there is money.

Everywhere You Solve A Problem There Is Honor.

Years ago, my secretary called and said, "Dr. Murdock, the couple that normally takes you to the airport doesn't want to take you Tomorrow. They want to go shopping. Can you drive yourself to the airport?"

I felt so violated I said, "I can drive all of you to the airport. I can pay all of your way out of Dallas."

I am so glad I am saved. I do not think I would last 8 days on the streets without the controlling power of The Holy Spirit. God did not make everybody I have met. I know that in my heart.

I called a little lady who had 4 children. Three were triplets. I asked, "Alice, would you Mind taking me to the airport Tomorrow?"

Let me tell you what she did not say.

She did not say, "What time?"

She did not say, "If you let me know ahead of time. This is a little bit last minute, you know? I have 4 kids, Dr. Murdock."

She did not say, "I will have to check and see if I have gas in my car. How far is it, Dr. Murdock?"

She did not say, "Could somebody else do it?"

She did not say, "What is wrong with the people

who normally take you?"

There is not a human on earth that is not creative. Not one. Do you want to see how creative somebody is? Give them an instruction and see how many ways they can find to get out of it. It is like the genius of Lucifer appears.

She said, "Oh, it would be an Honor, Dr. Murdock. It would be an Honor." So she started taking me to the airport.

Some of the staff did not like it because she was a girl. Why would a guy want another guy to hang around him if he was really a guy?

"Dr. Murdock, we do not think it looks good."

I said, "Does it look good for me to be on the freeway? That does not look good either."

One week I told her, "Alice, I am flying all night from Los Angeles and I would rather get a taxi because you have the children and I will arrive before 6am."

"Oh, I would not dream of a man of God riding in a taxi," she said.

"Alice, there is nothing sinful about riding in a taxi."

She was there.

As I walked out of a meeting, somebody handed me two $100.00 bills and said, "Do anything you want to with it."

I got off the plane and said, "Alice, somebody gave me two $100.00 bills and said I can do anything I want with them. Buy the kids some school supplies."

A few weeks later, somebody handed me five $100.00 bills on my way out of the church. They, too, said, "Do what you want with it."

Whoever tells you money doesn't make you feel

good, they're fools. I always feel better when I have money. Don't you feel better? I feel God when I see a $100.00 bill.

I got off the plane and said, "Alice, somebody gave me five $100.00 bills. Go buy you some clothes."

Whoever told you that all the money God gives you was meant to feed somebody down the street is ludicrous. They say, "I am just blessed to be a blessing."

Does that take away the pain of being blessed? Does that make you feel holy?

When I give money to my son, I do not want him going up and down the street handing it to everybody. When I give money to my mother, I did not want her to give it to grandkids I did not like.

Do you remember the episode where God removed Lot from Abraham's life? After they separated God said to Abraham, "I want to talk to you about My plans. Now that that guy's gone, I want to show you what I am giving you. It stretches as far as you can see, and reaches as far as you can walk."

He did not say, "Go get a school bus, find 50 other poor people, split up the land, and drive everyone there."

1.   Men Stay Poor Because They Feel Guilty Over The Blessing.

2.   Men Stay Poor Because They Feel Guilty Over The Goodness of God.

3.   Men Stay Poor Because They Feel Unworthy of Any Blessing of Any Open Door God Gives Them.

One day her car broke down. I said, "Alice, what kind of car have you always loved?"

"Oh, Dr. Murdock."

Was that a Miracle? I do not think so. It is called a Reward System.

She solved a problem for me, and I solved hers. Do you really have to go on a 21 day fast to understand that? Do you have to fall out in the Spirit and foam at the mouth to understand that? Is this thing a mystery?

Ephesians 6:8 could not be clearer: *Any Good Thing I Do For Another Human, That Is The Experience God Will Schedule For Me.* Hallelujah! If I want something to happen in my life, I just have to make it happen for somebody else.

4. Men Stay Poor Because They Have Never Inventoried The Divine Difference Within Them.

5. Men Stay Poor Because They Do Not Care Enough To Be Attentive.

I am not a smart man. I refuse to take any IQ test. I want to live thinking I am a lot smarter than what I really am. I do not want to know the truth about my brain.

I am not a smart man, but I am an attentive man. I know that anything I want has been *hidden* in my environment.

I know there is something I am not seeing, so I look and I look until I see.

Servanthood Guarantees Access To Greatness.

Through problem-solving I can tap into any environment I want to enter. I was talking with Jesse Duplantis today, a long-time friend I was raised with.

I had completely forgotten about something he reminded me of today. He said, "Mike, my whole ministry is because of your daddy. Your daddy came to Franklin and won my grandma to Jesus."

I remembered Daddy picking her up. We all sat in the back with his grandma, going to church. She did not have a way to church.

Jesse said, "She was saved under your daddy's ministry. She won my daddy and mama to Christ. I would not even have a ministry had it not been for J. E. Murdock."

I said, "Jesse, I forgot all about that."

You are 4 people away from any human on the earth. I had a bunch of preachers call me from overseas and say, "We have been trying to get in touch with Jesse Duplantis. We would pay any amount of money to have him. Could you possibly help us contact him? Would you put in a good word with him for us?"

"Yes, if I like you I will put in a good word." I am 4 humans away from any other human on the earth. I can access any Future.

When You Solve A Problem, You Create A Favorable Memory. It becomes a lifetime well of blessing. You could have solved a problem 20 years ago. Even after you are dead, the Mephibosheths of your family still get to talk to David. Hallelujah.

Myles Monroe and I sat in England about to board a plane to go to Ghana. A man walked through the turnstile.

Brother Monroe said, "Do you know him?"

I said, "No, who is he?"

"He is the third greatest soccer player in the world."

I do not follow soccer, so I did not know him. The man walked over, and hugged Myles. Myles said, "I want you to meet Mike Murdock."

He said, "Oh, I know Mike. I have all your books."

Then he hugged me.

Everybody was getting on the plane. He said, "I will be right back." He took off and left us sitting there. Finally, he came through the turnstiles. He walked over with a bag full of English money...Sterling pounds. A pound is worth about two dollars.

He said, "Mike, I cannot be around you without planting some Seed. I have read your books. They have changed my life." Then he started handing money to me.

I started stuffing it in each of my pockets. I had pounds in my briefcase, and in all of my pockets. I sat there thinking, "Customs is going to think this is drug money, as sure as the world. They will think I am carrying drugs." My pockets were so stuffed with cash I waddled as I walked.

The Holy Spirit spoke to me and made it so clear. He said, "I can get money to you anywhere you are."

"Well, Brother Mike, preachers talk so much about money."

Do they talk as much about it as you look for it? Have you ever heard a sermon as long as the 8 hours that you work for money? You've worked for money 100 times longer than you have ever listened to any preacher.

Isn't it kind of idiotic to work 40 hours, drive in traffic, and stay mad at your boss because he doesn't give you extra money? Isn't it even more idiotic to get angry when a preacher gets up on Sunday morning and says, "I want to pray the blessing of the Lord over your finances, and as you bring your Tithe, God's going to multiply it."

My greatest fear of hell has been being with all the

idiots in one place at one time.

Why Do Men Stay Poor?

6. Men Stay Poor Because They Will Not Listen To Men Who Have Money.

7. Men Stay Poor Because They Do Not Ask Questions On How To Improve Their Lot In Life.

8. Men Stay Poor Because They Ignore The Problems Closest To Them.

9. Men Stay Poor Because They Will Not Listen To An Instruction Their Boss Gives Them. He has to give the instruction 4 times and they lose Favor.

10. Men Stay Poor Because They Do Not Celebrate Favor.

Favor is irreplaceable.

Everything you do adds Favor or removes it. You are like a bank account, and every time you follow an instruction, you add to your bank account. Every time you do not, you take money out of your bank account.

How do you react to Favor?

How do you react to Opportunity?

Everything From God Is Camouflaged As An Opportunity.

God has never written you a check, has He? Yet, you tell everybody how good God has been to you. You cannot even show me a check He has written you, can you?

God blesses us through people. What kind of person? *The person you serve.*

The person you serve is the only person authorized to be a part of your financial equation.

Every one of us has a best friend, and he has not

given you 10 percent of what your boss has given you. Why is he your best friend?

Your boss has given you 100 times more money than your best friend has. Think on that.

How do you respond when there is Favor?

Either this Gospel works, or it is fraudulent.

If Prosperity is evil, why are we working?

If money is going to kill you, why do you carry it everywhere?

If money makes you get away from God, why doesn't the devil wake you up in the morning with money all over your bedroom?

The last two and a half years have been the roughest of my life, but God's bringing me through it.

They have been the roughest two and a half years of my lifetime, mainly because of my personal disappointment in humans where I made an investment. I felt like everything in my life was crazy, wrong, stupid and dumb. I hated every book I had ever written.

Week after week I felt nothing. I would go through magazines trying to find something to trigger energy. Nothing. Zero. I wanted to die. I stayed in bed until 3:00 in the afternoon; as long as I possibly could.

I would call my sister, Deborah, to represent me to the staff. I said, "Sis, I believe I could lose my Mind."

I was studying my pain instead of my inspiration; studying where I failed with people.

I was building an extension to my house. Buck Avanzini, who built The Wisdom Center, presented a bill for tens of thousands of dollars to add all the wood to my 5,600 square foot house. I stood out there and said, "This is nuts. This is crazy. I am only one man. It is stupid for me to build something like this."

The Holy Spirit spoke to me, "Do you think this is splendor? You think this is palatial? You think your house is nice? This is what World-Class is to you?" Then I realized God had a little higher standard than Swanee Street, in Lake Charles, Louisiana.

I told Buck, "Go ahead, build it."

"Where is the money?"

"I do not know. Just build it."

I flew to England to speak and when I was through speaking to 10,000 people The Holy Spirit said, "Sign autographs for 10 or 15 minutes."

So I told the people, "I normally do not do this, but I am going to autograph my books for the next 10 or 15 minutes."

When I was through signing books, as I was walking back through all the thousands of people, a man walked up to me, put his arms around me and hugged my neck. He did not say a word. I held him for a few seconds. He is a wonderful man of God from overseas.

I went back to a little side room. I was sitting there. God had given me just enough anointing to feed the people present, but not enough to feed me. There is a different anointing for you than there is for other people.

The anointing for a ministry is not for you. That is why you feel emptied when you have preached. God gives you an anointing to feed His family, but you must know Him on a different level for God to feed you.

As I was sitting there, Brother Ron Bowman walked in and said, "The man who just hugged you said to give you this." Afterward, we began to count that money. It was a stack of $100.00 bills.

In that envelope, from 10,000 miles away, was the exact amount of odd numbered money that paid for all of that extension. All 5,600 feet of wood.

God said, "I can get money to you anywhere you are."

I would not work for a poor God, and I would not trust a lying God.

You do not have to be broke.

You do not have to stay poor.

You do not have to drive an old car.

You do not have to live in the corner of somebody's house. You have a Jehovah-jireh.

"If ye then, being evil, know how to give good gifts unto your children, how much more shall your Father which is in Heaven give good things to them that ask Him?" (Matthew 7:11). Hallelujah.

You can talk about the God that killed Ananias and Sapphira for lying. You can talk about the God that opened up the earth for Korah. You can talk about the God that let she bears come out and eat 42 children who disrespected a prophet of God.

I have met the God of Deuteronomy 28; the God of Malachi 3; the God of Luke 6:38, and Mark 10.

I have met the 100-fold God Who says, "Anything you put in My hands will come back to you 100-fold."

I believed Him then.

I still believe Him right now.

☙ 6 ❧

TIME - THE DIVINE CURRENCY

Something Happens In God's Presence That Cannot Happen Anywhere Else.

"Father, we thank You for the privilege of access to You. We are very, very comfortable with Your Love and with Your Presence. We are Receivers: Receivers of the Blood of Christ...Receivers of The Holy Spirit... Receivers of an Anointing upon our life...Receivers of our Difference...Receivers of Your Assignment upon our life; and we have focused on the part of You that You wish all of us understood and that is the character of God, and we embrace Your character.

"We pray a special grace...a special anointing on us as we receive Your Word. Bring all things to our remembrance this day. Let this be the beginning of the happiest seasons we have ever walked into in our entire lifetime. In Jesus' Name. Amen."

I was talking to Dr. Bob Rogers the other day. I consider him the number one authority on fasting and prayer. He was on a 100-day fast. He just finished a 21-day fast with his church. Many of his people do 40-day fasts.

He said that whenever a group is fasting for the same focus, *whoever* in the group gets a breakthrough in that circle, gets it for *everyone*. If someone has a breakthrough for their home or household salvation, everyone on that fast receives the same.

It is much easier to sit on your bed on a Wednesday night and flip a remote control to watch the service. That is far easier than getting dressed then driving an hour to get to church, and then drive back an hour and to end up getting home late. You may be thinking, surely there is an easier way to go to church. But, there is something special that happens when you enter the House of the Lord; and this is why I left my home tonight and why we put focus on this.

The focus of this book is *Why Men Stay Poor.*

It is not a tirade or an accusation against poverty or poor people. There is a reason for poverty...and according to the Bible, it comes through our decisions. According to Proverbs 13:18, poverty and shame cometh to him that refuseth instruction.

Everywhere the Bible references obedience, you see a reference to blessing and Prosperity. Obedience and Prosperity are connected. It took me a lifetime to understand why. My father is a precious, spirit-filled, holy and righteous man. When I went to Bible School, he did not have the $4.00 a day I needed to pay my way. Bible School was approximately $4.00 a day; $550.00 for a semester at Southwestern Assemblies of God Bible College.

How can a holy, righteous man, totally committed to God, who prays 4 to 10 hours a day, stay poor? There is no relationship between the love of God and your Prosperity. His love is unqualified, but Prosperity has to be qualified for. You do not have to do anything to be loved, but you have to do something to birth increase in your life.

I believe in the blessing of the Lord. I like the word *Prosperity*. I do not like the word impoverished.

I am not poor. I do not want to be poor. I have been poor, and the best thing I can do for the poor is not be one of them. A person who cannot swim cannot help somebody who is drowning.

I have not met very many poor people who were teachable. I have a desire to nurture somebody financially. Every day I study and think on how to maximize a moment.

The number one Divine currency God gave you was not money, or even health; but He gave you *time*. Wealthy men do not have more time than poor men, but I have never met a poor man who cared about his time.

I remember people dropping by my father's house. They would sit there and talk, stealing 3 hours of his time. Why? Time meant nothing. I have never met a poor man who valued time.

Time Is The Number One Currency God Gave You.
Your Reaction To Time Is A Prediction of Your Financial Future.

Take a 10-pound bar of iron. If I make horse shoes out of it, I make $30.00. If I make needles, I make $300.00. If I make watch springs, I make $3,000.00.

Time-Management Is One of The Key Ingredients To Prosperity. If you want to make $1 million a year, your time will be worth $500.00 an hour. You have 52 weeks in a year, with two weeks off for vacation.

Remember that *Rest Is A Command.*

God considered rest equal with anything else He created. He gave us an example. (Read Genesis 2:2.)

If you have 50 work weeks a year, working 40

hours a week, that is 2,000 work hours in a year. If you make $10.00 an hour, that is $20,000.00...$20.00 an hour, that is $40,000.00...$50.00 an hour, that is $100,000.00 a year.

Look at your time. You trade time for everything else you want. *Time Is Currency*.

1. Men Stay Poor Because They Have Never Inventoried Divine Deposits In Them.

They have never looked at something God placed in them. What do you have that is uncommon? What do you have to trade?

I said to one of the men who works for me, "You are not being rewarded for your knowledge and there is a reason for it. You work here on the staff. You make good money, but you are not going to make what you could. You do not have to leave the ministry to make it. You are not being rewarded for your knowledge. *Knowledge Has A Value*."

"In the time you take to teach one of our staff members for 30 minutes, you could have a video tape and put it on your website. Make that 30-minute video available for $20.00. If a thousand people purchase the video, that is $20,000.00."

What do you know that others need to know?

What do you have that others crave? Inspiration.

Why does Zig Zigler get $30,000.00 to speak for one hour? When I first heard that, I said, "That is crazy. Nobody is worth $30,000.00 per hour." But, he spoke to 10,000 men; 10,000 businessmen who went out and raised their sales by 20-30 percent; and they got Zig to do that for $3.00 a person. Imagine if you handed a man $3.00, and his sales jumped $30,000.00 that year. *Duh!*

I see myself as a poor man who became blessed. Was it luck? I do not think so. Is it a mystery? No. Was it a Miracle? Not as little as I pray for money. I do not pray about money. I do not consider money a Miracle.

Do you think that when I see Donald Trump I see an intercessor?

Warren Buffett would not pay $400.00 to help his sister when she was behind on her apartment rent. Do you think I see generosity when I look at him? Do I see the power or the presence of God? Absolutely not. I see a man who applied laws...The Laws of God.

"Wisdom is the principal thing; therefore get Wisdom: and with all thy getting get understanding. Exalt her, and she shall promote thee: she shall bring thee to honour," (Proverbs 4:7-8).

Men and women want two different things. Men want *significance*. Women want *security*. Those are the two basic needs of humans. Why do you think people paint their hair purple and red? Is it because they love purple and red? No. *Notice me.* There is a passion in every human to become important to *somebody*.

Not everybody, but *somebody*.

Mary Kay Ash was worth $300 million and her company $1.2 billion at her death. She made the statement, "Imagine every person you meet wearing a sign saying, 'Please tell me I am important.'"

Men want *significance*. Women want *security*. Both are satisfied through the Wisdom of God.

"She shall give to thine head an ornament of grace: a crown of glory shall she deliver to thee. I have taught thee in the way of Wisdom; I have led thee in right paths. When thou goest, thy steps shall not be straitened; and when thou runnest, thou shalt not stumble. Take fast hold of instruction," (Proverbs 4:9, 11-13).

Instruction is not training. The difference in men is the instruction they are able to follow. The poor are less likely to follow instructions...*to follow Divine Laws.* One of the Divine Laws that I consider important is *The Law of Adaptation.* There is a reason why the dinosaur is not here, but the cockroach is.

Adaptation.

You are not ready for your Future or you would be there. How do you adapt to the Future you are designing in your life?

"Thy steps shall not be straitened; and when thou runnest, thou shalt not stumble. Take fast hold of instruction...for she is thy life," (Proverbs 4:12-13).

Of all the things God could have talked about, He just talked to us about the blessing of the Lord in Deuteronomy 28. Twenty percent of what Christ talked about was money. He talked more about money than He did prayer and faith combined. Is money important to God? *It must be.*

Deuteronomy 28 starts off with "if." The word "if" appears 331 times in the Scriptures. The Bible is not a book about destiny. The Bible is a book about *decisions.* You are *designed* for success, but you are not *pre-destined* for success.

Destiny is what happens without your participation. Destiny is a Divine decision; not a human decision. One of the most important things about the Wisdom of God is distinguishing between a human decision or a God decision.

Isaiah 1:17 instructs us to, "Learn to do well."

"If thou shalt hearken diligently unto the voice of the Lord thy God, to observe and to do all His commandments," (Deuteronomy 28:1).

If you take the letter "U" out of the alphabet, you lose 3,000 words in your vocabulary. *Everything God makes is a part.* Nothing God makes is complete. Your eyes need to view. Your Mind needs thoughts. Your ear needs sound. Your mouth needs words.

Everything God made is a part. Water is H_2O; two parts hydrogen and one part oxygen. If you double the oxygen, it is now hydrogen peroxide...which will kill you.

When you take something out of the equation you change the outcome.

A young man said to me one night, "I heard every word you said. I did everything you said, but it did not happen for me the way it did for you."

I replied, "You did not know what I did not say. You added some ingredients. This is what I said and this is what you decided to add to the equation." When you change the equation, you change the outcome.

"And all these blessings shall come on thee...if thou shalt hearken unto the voice of the Lord thy God. Blessed shalt thou be in the city, and blessed shalt thou be in the field. Blessed shall be the fruit of thy body, and the fruit of thy ground, and the fruit of thy cattle, the increase of thy kine, and the flocks of thy sheep," (Deuteronomy 28:2-4).

Isn't this amazing? He said if you obey Me even your animals will become supernatural lovers and multiply.

"Blessed shall be thy basket and thy store. Blessed shalt thou be when thou comest in, and blessed shalt thou be when thou goest out. The Lord shall cause thine enemies that rise up against thee to be smitten before thy face: they shall come out against thee one way, and flee before thee seven ways. The Lord shall command the blessing upon thee in thy storehouses," (Deuteronomy 28:5-8).

Is God the God of excess? *Obviously.*

Look at all the animals. Look at all the stars. What we think is excess, God thinks is a start. God is nothing like us. You need to understand that. We are made in His image, but He is far beyond.

"The Lord shall make thee plenteous in goods... The Lord shall open unto thee His good treasure, the Heaven to give...," (Deuteronomy 28:11-12).

The Heaven to give... The Bible is a book about *receiving.* God said to Adam, I want you to receive a garden. (See Genesis 2:8.) I want you to receive Eve. (See Genesis 2:22.) "He came unto His own, and His own received Him not," (John 1:11).

Nobody has everything God gave them.

They only have what they were *capable* of receiving. Almost every Divine gift God gave you has *never* been opened. Have you ever seen a child so carried away with one gift that they forgot the other 10 on the other side of the tree?

2. Men Stay Poor Because They Do Not Understand The Character of God.

The worst thing about being single is the absence of somebody to give to, because the need to give surpasses the need to receive. *There is more pleasure in watching another happy.* That is why parents sit proudly around the Christmas tree watching their children jumping around the Christmas tree excited about their presents feeling, I am so glad I made this happen for them. That is why The Bible indicates it is more pleasurable to give than it is to receive. (See Acts 20:35.)

What comes first? Giving or receiving? *Obviously giving.* How can you give if you have not received?

Your life begins with receiving.

You receive *the breath of God.*

You receive *the life of God.*

You receive *invisible gifts, talents and skills.*

You receive *affection.*

You receive *love.*

You receive *attention.*

You receive *medical help.*

You enter the world receiving.

Do you *know* the character of God?

Do you *understand* the character of God?

I was thumbing through a catalog and saw a woman wearing a beautiful fur. I said, "Wow. It would be nice to have a wife to give something like that to." But I turned the pages and saw a beautiful green jade; now that I have been single 33 years, and I said, "Wow that would be nice to be married to have a wife to buy that for."

Suddenly The Holy Spirit spoke to me and said, "Now you know how I feel. I have a whole universe to give away." Now if giving creates ecstasy, can you imagine how excited God gets when He finds somebody capable of receiving?

Your ability to receive excites God.

I found out one of my sisters had always wanted a Corvette. I did not know that. Been my sister for 50 something years, and she got all excited. She was real excited and trying to get some pennies, and I said, "Oh, Sis. That is easy. That is all you want is a Corvette? That is easy to make happen." I was excited.

I found out my sister Deborah liked the Hummer. I said, "Oh, Sis. That is easy to make happen."

Once you understand the character of God and that we are made in His image, we have a nature to give...*to bless.*

No man would stay poor if he knew how exciting it was to give. That is the whole point of receiving... *become capable of the highest ecstasy which is giving.*

Our goal in being prosperous is not to collect pieces of paper with a dead man's picture. Somebody says money will not make you happy. *What you do with money is what makes you happy.* Duh.

You can bless people. You can create so many experiences for others. That is the Divine role of Prosperity. *Money creates experiences for other people.*

Do you understand the character of God?

3. Men Stay Poor Because They Have Never Inventoried Divine Deposits In Them.

Do you know what God has put inside of you? What is your Divine difference from another?

Your Success Depends On Your Difference.

Pastor Holton did not marry Jackie because she reminded him of an old girlfriend. No, she was not like anybody else.

Do you go to McDonald's because it reminds you of Whataburger?

You must know your difference. Can you tell me your difference in a sentence? Do you know your difference from everybody else?

Never study your weakness; study your difference.

What makes you unlike another?

Attentiveness to detail? Are you good in mechanics? Are you an encourager? What do you have? Are you accuracy-oriented?

If you do not notice detail, maybe you are a cheerful person. When you walk in a room, you energize the room. You may be good at details and study or you may be a cheerful energizer that when you go in a room just your presence excites.

Do you know your difference? Do you know the difference of people around you? Have you identified their Divine contribution to your life? Do you know why God put somebody in your life? Do you know their Divine contribution to you?

Everything You Do Not Have Is Hidden In Somebody God Put Close To You.

There are 3 levels of passion. Ask. Seek. Knock. (See Matthew 7:7.) *Ask* means something is close. *Seek* means it is out of your realm of comfort. *Knock* means somebody is trying to hide what God has for you.

4.   Men Stay Poor Because They Had No Big Dreams.

Desires Birth Discovery.

When you want something, you figure out a way to get it. Remember Genesis 15:5..? "Abraham, see the stars? That is what your kids are going to be like." Designate a dream wall, or a Tomorrow room where you have pictures of your Future. I used to put 12 book covers in January so that I had a book for every month. I printed a quarter of a million so that I would be inspired and look at that wall and say that is my next book. When I saw a book cover, I became motivated to get it written.

Where is your dream wall? If I walked in your home, would it be a museum? Do you have pictures of just yesterday? Some people are excited about yesterday. I am not.

A single picture of your Future is worth more than all the past pictures of your life.

God is constantly creating. Creation is not a conclusion...it is a continuous beginning. Remember God's obsession with new. He said, "Even My mercies are new every morning," (see Lamentations 3:23).

If I walked into your home, would I see pictures of the dream of Tomorrow? I often tell about the young bellman who carried people's luggage to their hotel room, but under the glass, he held a picture of the most famous hotel in the world, and every morning he would say, "Some day I will own this hotel. They are giving me quarters and nickels and dimes, but someday I will own this hotel."

When You Decide What You Want, The Method For Obtaining It Becomes Clear.

When you decide what you want, how to get it becomes obvious. Every thought is pregnant. It has a parade of children. That is why I document my thoughts daily keeping a recorder with me constantly because the highest Honor to God is to document when He talks to you.

Something God tells you will birth wealth.

Something God instructs you will birth increase and multiplication or the correction of your course. The anointing does not birth discerning. *Divine words birth discerning.*

How do you handle God's conversation about your Future? Why did God give Abraham a picture of his

Future?

The young bellman eventually became the owner of that hotel. Everywhere I go I stay in his hotels. His name was Conrad Hilton. He had a picture of a Future.

God wants to do business through you. We have 37 millionaires so far through our ministry. My goal is for 300 people to become kingdom millionaires...*that God will do business through us on the earth.* We will give birth to visions and dreams...books and missions and colleges, TV stations and radio stations. If you have trouble thinking of the blessing, you have locked into poverty thinking.

What have poor people accomplished? Even poor people, whether it was Gandhi or Mother Teresa – they had some people who felt guilty for never doing anything and they supported them financially.

What are *your dreams?*

What are *your goals?*

What do you consider *a blessed life?*

I consider a home where there is safety to be a blessing and a need. I consider being able to send my son through school or college a blessing.

5. Men Stay Poor Because They Have Never Identified Who God Is Using To Bless Them.

Out of all the humans on the earth, identify the one that writes you a check every week or twice a month or whatever the case may be. Not one of your relatives gives you a check as often as your boss. Your best friend probably has not written you a check in months.

Have you identified who God has chosen to create a financial stream into your life?

Have you identified the top 10 sponsors of your life? Who are the top investors in your life? And are they profiting from their investment? Who has invested time in you? Who has invested correction and mentorship in you? Who has invested money in you?

What has been their return?

How do you handle your investors? If they give you a hundred dollars for your birthday, do you say it could have been $200.00? What's the last thing said on Christmas morning, "Is this all?"

If God is the number one investor in you, what is He getting out of the investment? Have you identified your investors in your life? And how have you documented gratitude?

Your father taught you to walk, talk, go to school. He gave you everything with no return on it for years; and now you think when you throw him a hundred dollar bill you have really blessed him?

I tell my staff to think of everybody they know who writes as many checks as I do, and I laughingly say, "So I is the man." If I am writing you more checks than anybody else or there is nobody else in your life who is writing you checks, I should be in your equation. What I say should be in your equation. My joy should make a difference to you. It would be to your advantage for me to like you.

The Difference In Seasons Is Who Enjoys You. I cannot change your life but you should change who likes you. Every time you solve a problem for someone, you prove Honor. *Everywhere There Is Honor There Is Favor.*

Favor is a passion someone has to invest in you. Everywhere there is Favor, there is money. You may have a friend that if they died Tomorrow, you would not miss them a day. There are others who if they left, your whole world would change.

Wisdom Is The Ability To Recognize Difference. Difference in value, difference in people, difference in purpose, difference in function, difference in the environment.

What are your dreams and what are your goals? May this season be the happiest season of your financial Prosperity...financial blessing.

You have to have the Mind of Christ God has deposited into your dreams and goals. The Wisdom Center is debt-free...paid for. I have gone to churches where they think an answer to a prayer is being able to borrow money. I think an answer to a prayer is to be able to lend money and make money off of it.

One day my banker asked me, "Why don't you ever borrow money."

I replied, "I do not need it."

I have been going to banks lately that do not even have as much money as I do because they cannot cash my checks. They say they have to order the money. I have had more in my briefcase than they have been able to cash.

You Can Only Conquer Something You Hate.

If you do not hate being broke, you will stay broke.

Never Complain About Something You Permit. What You Can Tolerate You Cannot Change.

Develop a hatred for poverty.

Nurture a passion for God to do business through you. Maybe you are thinking that God can only do business through a preacher. Did you know some preachers are broke? Being a preacher does not make you have money. If anything it might be the opposite. Go to the credit bureau and the worst people on earth to pay their bills are preachers. They probably subconsciously think that Jesus is about to come so they borrow as much as they can.

6.   Men Stay Poor Because They Misinterpret Experiences In Their Life.

My father built 7 churches. He had 7 children. He prayed. He sought God. He was an honest man. He was a loving man. Passionate for God, but he had no money. He was gifted. He could lay brick. Let me tell you an event in my father's life that kept him broke.

When he started his ministry, a man asked him to work 4 days for $2.00 a day. At the end of the 4 days, the man gave him $8.00.

My dad had developed a sore of some kind on his hand so went to the doctor and had it lanced. The doctor said he would normally charge $35.00 for this, but decided to charge my father only $8.00. My father interpreted that event that it was wrong for him to receive money for any work. Every time he would tell me he would say, "Why did not he say $10.00? Why did not he say $7.00?" We always think there is something Divine about every number.

My father could build anything, but he would never take a penny. People would offer, but he would not take it because God spoke to him through that $8.00 event.

7.   Men Stay Poor Because They Resent The Wealthy.

You Cannot Learn From Someone You Resent.

If you pass by a big house thinking, "Well, I wonder whose money they took for that?"

Instead, be like George Foreman who saw a big house and said to his mother, "Mama, someday I am going to give you a house just like that."

If you do not admire people who have achieved there is no hope of you having a great Future.

I carry a Nook eReader everywhere I go. It holds 3,200 books that I have with me at all times. I consider my Mind to be my greatest asset. My Mind is my garden.

Your Mind Is Where You Grow The Fruit For Your Future. Your Mind is your world. Your world is in your Mind. Everything every billionaire has ever had written, including Aristotle Onassis; who explains what he would do if he had $3.00 left to his name.

There are no advantages in poverty. If poverty was wonderful, don't you think God would guarantee it? Some say they know people who backslid because they made a lot of money. I know people who had no money and backslid. *I know people who drowned, but I still drink water.*

Aristotle Onassis, the billionaire, the tycoon from Greece who married Jacqueline Kennedy, said that if he had $3.00 left to his name, the first thing he would do would not be to go to a cheap café and have a meal. He would go to the most luxurious hotel in the city and buy a cup of coffee because the people he wanted in his Future are in that environment.

Who do you learn from?

When you are watching TV late at night and a woman comes on who weighs 350 pounds then shares that she took a certain pill and that was her result. Will you reach for the phone and buy her pills? Would you learn from somebody who is bankrupt? You can if they have gone through it like Donald Trump. I read every word Donald Trump ever said. He has some fascinating thoughts – which are actually Scriptural laws.

I read the investment rules by Warren Buffett. One of them was, never invest in something you do not want to know a lot about.

I did. Invested $30,000.00 in oil. I did not know anything. Just liked the people who sold it to me. They were on the board of a famous preacher and I believed them. *Lost every penny.*

I keep this little Nook with me. I also have the Kindle Fire because I can download a book for almost half price and keep every book I want right there. One of the rewards of listening to right people is inspiration.

You Cannot Fail If You Learn How To Keep Yourself Inspired. It is impossible to fail if you learn how to keep yourself excited. It was the secret of Thomas Edison. We fail when we lose inspiration. Failing to realize something that Napoleon Hill said over and over, that hidden in every adversity is an equal benefit.

Hidden In Every Loss Is Wisdom.

Everything that goes wrong in your life has hidden in it Divine gifts. Do not run away from pain. Look at what created it.

Who is your circle of counsel?

If your house is in foreclosure are you trying to get money or do you say something is wrong here? What should you be doing differently? A house is not worth saving. Your Mind is worth everything. You can buy a house every day of the week. You can buy houses without a down payment. You can buy a house and if you do not want to borrow money on it you can move in somebody's house and live for free.

Owning a house is not the end of the world.

Look at the homeless. Forty percent of them have a cell phone, but they do not have a home. They want a phone, they do not want a house. No taxes, no insurance.

Who do you learn from?

What are you learning?

How passionate are you about learning?

I consider the most important thing I do every day is not prayer. *The Most Important Thing I Do Every Day Is Ask Questions.*

If you do not ask questions you will not even know God. It is a question that leads you to God.

Jesus loved questions so much He answered questions with questions.

What are the last 3 questions you have asked yourself financially? Who do you learn from? What should you be learning? What questions should you be asking?

Cullen Davis who 30 years ago had a $12 million home. In fact me and Dr. Paul Yonggi Cho was walking out of his house one night. Cullen Davis who was known for a lot of things but he was a very wealthy man...one of the wealthiest men in Dallas.

Dr. Cho said, "This is the nicest home."

I said, "Man, it is like a museum." I had never seen a home like that in my lifetime and we were talking about how incredible it was. This was 30 years ago. I was 36.

I went to supper with Cullen more than once and I said, "How did you get your money? Tell me." I do not want him to write me a check. Don't throw me a fish. Show me the ocean you have been fishing in.

I said, "What is the most important thing I need to know about money?" He said, "Well, the first thing you need to know is information. Information...that is the first thing you look for."

How do you get information?

Asking questions. Asking questions of yourself. You do not have to have somebody around to ask questions.

Sometimes I will do little exercises for myself. If I had $1,000.00 left to my name what would I do with it? What are 3 things I can do with $1,000.00? How can I spend $1,000.00 and make $10,000.00?

Do I think about money? Every day of my life. Every day of my life. Why? It is a creator. Money buys equipment, prints Bibles.

8. Men Stay Poor Because They Do Not Think Money Is A Blessing. They have convinced themselves that money is for crooked people and that money will not help you. We sell ourselves on a philosophy that creates change or comfort.

If I am in a wheelchair I want to believe in healing. I want to see a Miracle so I go to Benny Hinn's services 5 times, and nothing happens so I change my philosophy to comfort me. Sometimes God wants you sick because that philosophy gives me comfort. Every one of us are living off the fruit of our belief system.

Your Belief System Has Created Your Circumstances.

Whatever you believe has created the world in which you live. Let me remind you that everybody's world is different. What I see on TV has never happened in my life. Did you know I have never seen a riot?

But if you watch TV it looks like that is what happens, and nothing in my life has ever happened on TV. What I see every day in my world I have never seen on TV so nobody lives in the same world. My Mind has created my world.

Focus Creates Your Feelings.

What do you consider the Divine gift inside of you? Is it discerning? Is it the willingness to work? Who do you learn from? Who do you learn from? Who are you willing to learn from? Whose advice do you pursue? Who do you admire?

Those Without A Financial Hero Do Not Have A Financial Future.

Do you remember when Warren Buffett wanted to learn from Benjamin Graham, I think it was in New York, and he was willing to drive all the way from Nebraska to sit at his feet? He did not even know what he was going to be paid. All he knew is that man understood investment like no man he had ever seen, and he decided to learn from the best there was. He was willing to learn for free.

Remember me saying that Oral Roberts told me he had a young man spend two hours with him and never ask him a single question about Divine healing?

I will never forget in Houston, Texas, I was preaching for a pastor and he was losing his church. In fact, the next day he was losing his church...losing everything. That night as I walked out the door he said, "Brother Mike, do you mind if somebody else drives you to the airport Tomorrow morning because I have a lot of things to do?"

I replied, "I do not mind at all."

I went and got in the car and I thought, "What an

idiot. Here he is, can't even make a church note." Could somebody else drive me to the airport? Never asked a single question. Oh, my greatest fear of going to hell has been with the fools in one place and not one decent sound for eternity.

Nobody can make the decisions for your life but you. What is the proof you want to learn about money? If I go into your house and I see a $100,000.00 house and 10 books on money I am not going to think you have much passion.

What is the proof that you want financial intelligence? Are you waiting for a ship to come in? Are you living by hope? It will not change unless you change it.

Do you think everything works out for the good? Do you think everything ends up working right? Go tell it to the people in the funeral homes. Tell that to a person dying with cancer.

Who inspires you to achieve your highest level? I am not talking about being a multimillionaire. I am talking about prospering where you can do what God told you to do.

In Isaiah 1:17, God says learn to do well. Hosea 4:6 says my people are destroyed for lack of knowledge.

We are not destroyed because of so many demons and devils. We are destroyed because we do not learn and we do not know. You cannot change your life until you change a day because your day is a life. You cannot change your life until you change something you do daily.

Routine Is The Road To Your Future.

Prosperous People Do Daily What The Poor Do Occasionally.

Your daily routine has everything to do with your financial knowledge and your intelligence. I want 4 bids for anything over $200.00 from 4 different companies. Did you know that I continuously have to battle that and have for years even with my staff?

I ask for 4 bids. Why? The fourth bid may be one-third of what everybody else charged. When I save 10 percent I add 10 percent to my salary figuratively speaking.

Do you negotiate? Do you want to know negotiation? Study Donald Trump's books, or study Paul's *26 Facts About Negotiation* in the book of Philemon.

Do you negotiate for everything? You never receive what you deserve in life. You receive what you negotiate for. Whatever you are willing to accept is where you are.

9. Men Stay Poor Because They Do Not Know How To Talk To Their Boss.

Credibility Is Currency.

Howard Hughes, whose life I studied closely, paid a man $500,000.00 a year. That was more than 45 years ago. He paid a man $500,000.00 a year just to pass paperwork under his hotel room door. That is all the man did. The man had a quality. The man was discreet and would not tell secrets. You say, "Man, he gets one-half of a million dollars a year just for saying nothing?" Well, go try to find that gift.

Go try to find somebody who can keep their mouth shut. Try to find them. You can find a dinosaur quicker than you can find that, but Howard Hughes was a recluse. He loved his privacy. He owned a hotel and would have the whole top floor as his penthouse, but he did not want anybody to find out who he was.

He did not want anybody to know who he was or where he was, and so this man was the only human on earth who knew where he was and he would pass all the business papers under the door, but this man could keep his mouth shut. He had a value. He had a quality.

How do you talk to a boss about a raise? Easy. How could you qualify for more than what you are receiving? What do you need to do to be worth more? What should you be doing differently?

Now your boss may say well one of the things that is a problem is you cause problems in every department he put you so you already used up half of your income. You are paid $12.00 an hour, but you are now worth $6.00 an hour to him because everywhere he puts you there is a problem. He has to be taken out of meetings to deal with you when his time is worth $150.00 a minute.

My bills are $9,000.00 an hour that comes out to about $150.00 a minute. When somebody wants to have a cup of coffee with me and says we need a good hour together. I will say, "Do I see $9,000.00?" I consider time my most precious quality. So when somebody wants to talk to me it needs to be to the point. It needs to be honest, with integrity. Make it precise and concise and I need to benefit from the conversation.

If a woman comes up to me after church and says, "Would you pray for me, my daughter has cancer. She is going to the hospital, nothing matters. That is all that matters." How are you benefitted? I am now releasing my anointing from the Lord to bring healing to that child and Miracles to her life. Now I am satisfied. I am not satisfied until I have fruit to every minute I spend. I have to feel that I maximize my hours.

I spoke 7 times one weekend in Miami. I was scheduled to speak to pastors. I had invested thousands of dollars in flying there so I could meet with other people. How do I maximize my hours? How do I make them count?

How do you talk to your boss? With respect, Honor? Do you ask him how you could improve what you do? What could you do differently? What are you doing wrong?

Very few people know how to talk to their own boss and how to make his time count. Be purposeful. How could you improve what you are doing? What should you change? What do you need to learn? Are you a burden? Do you cause stress? Do you cause agitation in any way?

If you do not have a Future there, he may say you are doing good because he will not care if you leave or if he sees you in his Future.

You must become time-conscious. Think, is there a quicker way to do this? *Thinking is not wasted time.* Remember Abraham Lincoln? He said if I have 4 hours to cut down a tree I would spend the first 3 sharpening the ax.

When you are given a task gather all the information needed at that moment. If there is something you do not know that is the time to ask the question.

I had a lady, and this happens actually a lot in my ministry, that I asked, "Did you get the task done?"

She said, "Well, you know I did not quite really understand what you said." Well, nobody ever tells me that.

I looked at it and said, "Uh, well why didn't you ask me?"

"Well, I went and asked so and so."

I said, "You went and asked someone who did not hear me or what I meant?"

"*Well,* I did not want to waste your time."

What a liar.

I said, "I gave you a job to do and you did not know how to do it and you let me think you were doing it."

I do not think wealthy men are anymore liars than poor men. In fact I believe the opposite. The more you lie the quicker you will lose.

Credibility and integrity is currency in my world.

Can you be trusted with an instruction? Can you be trusted with confidences? How do you react to a problem? What are your reactions to a problem?

When you talk to your boss tell him when you are wrong. "I missed it. I am sorry, I made a mistake."

The other day somebody said, "Uh, I made a mistake. Uh, I want to explain."

I said, "I do not want to hear why you did something stupid. I do not need to hear that. I do not have time to hear that. Just know what you did is stupid. Do not do it again."

"Well, I want to explain."

I said, "You do not have to explain stupid. You can't explain stupid. Just do what I said to do. Instructions are not training."

Instruction Is When Somebody Tells You What To Do. Training Is When They Explain Why.

It takes one year before any employee begins to make money for the company. One year.

Warren Buffett said it takes him two years to find an honest leader. It takes him two years to find a competent man to head one of his companies, and he has head hunters. A head hunter is somebody who looks for staff and leaders.

Where are your goals listed?

If I walk into your house do I see your goals? Are you in partnership with God? Are you trying to live a life without Him? Does His impressions matter to you?

I will never forget the day God gave me a plan in a real estate transaction and in 24 hours I added $4 million in my financial world in one day. I am not a smart man but I am an attentive man. I have not even earned the doctorate...it was honorary. I am not a smart man but I am an attentive man, and when somebody talks to me I listen.

I am a man very aware of my lack and that there is so much I do not know, and I admire people who have accomplished so much with their life. I study great men. I study achievers. I study their secrets.

I have read hours of Ronald Reagan's handwriting. What did he have? He had the ability to stay poised in the presence of fools. That is a genius. If you can stay non-responsive to an idiot you have got patience, you have got profound capabilities. If you can stay quiet when somebody comes against you.

I tweeted the other day, "Stay in the chariot and do not chase the peasant who throws tomatoes at you."

Stay at peace. Stay poised.

Learn what you can from others. Your goals need to be specific. Faith has to have precision.

Have you noticed every healing ministry that says somebody is being healed right now in your lower neck?

Somebody, there is one being healed in your lower back. Healings happen.

Clarity Creates Faith.

When you know what you want, your faith rises. What you can see you can produce.

I had a young man admit he wanted to make $50,000.00 a year. I said, "Why don't we move it to $52,000.00? Let's try to come up with $1,000.00 a week. I like solid stuff you know. Write that down. Now write the names of 5 people who do business with you, who believe in you, who like you. They are your investors."

Identify your circle of counsel. Those who give you advice. Who sees what you do not see? Who knows something you do not know? And remember one missing conversation changes the decision.

Is there any conversation you are missing in your life? What should you be talking about right now? What should you be looking at right now?

See yourself as a learner. See yourself as a financial student...a Financial Protégé. Since our church started, I have never taken one cent of the Tithe and Offerings. I do not want any man telling me what I should live on. I have a Jehovah-jireh and I trust Him.

I trust His leading. I trust His open doors. I trust His faith. If God likes me nothing else matters. When you pleasure the heart of God, He thinks of ways to bless you.

He said, "I will open the windows of Heaven and pour you out a blessing that you will not have room to receive it," (see Malachi 3:10).

God knows you and I need finances to live our life. There are well meaning Christian people who are anti-

Prosperity. They actually think the preacher is there talking to them about an Offering so he can buy himself a new tie. If a person does not know the power of money on the earth they do not qualify for it.

You Only Attract What You Respect.

I put a great value on the financial blessing because I see what can be done with it. We have a Jehovah-jireh who knows what we want to accomplish and what we want to do. The government can spend $500 million researching worms. People are worth a lot more than worms.

John wrote that He wanted you to prosper even as your soul would prosper. (See 3 John 2.) God said He wishes you were a thousand times more than what you are. (See Deuteronomy 1:11.)

Nothing takes care of itself. What you do with 24 hours determines what you become. Some years ago, I fasted 3 days a week, Monday, Tuesday and Wednesday; for two continuous years. During those two years God taught me profoundly. What He taught me about time was that every day of my life was like a train on a track and as long as I was making progress I generated pleasure.

Progress Creates Instant Pleasure.

You do not have to lose 50 pounds to feel pleasure. Lose two pounds and you will be on the phone telling someone about it. Your life is like a train on a track moving towards cities of accomplishment. You have 24 golden box cars. What you put in those box cars determines the speed and the distance your life moves. If you do not decide what goes in that box car or that hour, somebody else will decide what happens to your hour.

If you do not decide your vision...your goals... where your life is moving, somebody else will.

What are the decisions you should be making? Will you embrace the character of God? If you do not think God wants you to have money, your creativity will shut down. You will become hostile toward people who want you to assist them.

The most important thing to know in your life is the character of God. You do not need to know a lot of things about God. You just need to make a decision on what you want your life to be like.

What is an ideal lifestyle for you?

You need to identify the gifts of God inside of you. The gifts of God inside of you.

Make a decision how you will reward the investors in your life. How will you show them Honor.

Who are you willing to learn from? Make a decision to study for one hour a day on finances.

I go on TV to help other ministries in their part-nerships. I encourage their partners and show them what God will do for partnership...when they are linked with God. They will play that over and over so people who are not familiar with our ministry think that is all I do, yet not a penny of that goes for me.

A man said to me, "I heard you on TV and you talked for one hour about money. Why?"

I replied, "For the same reason you worked 40 hours to get some."

Never *trivialize* money. Never *belittle* it. A man said to me, "I am just not into that Prosperity message."

I responded, "Then why did you dive for the quarter on the pavement a few hours ago?"

Paul said, "The love of money is the root of all evil,"

(1 Timothy 6:10). He did not say money. He said, "The love of money." He did not say it was all evil. He said it is the root.

Who is God using right now in your life to bless you? Who has been good to you? Who *opens* the door for you?

Are you really in Partnership with God? If you are not a Tither, which is giving 10 percent of your income back to God, I have no hope for you. There is only one reason people do not Tithe. They really do not believe it. They really do not believe the 100-fold return.

A friend was talking to me about mutual funds. He said he found a company that consistently paid a 12-14 percent return consistently. Should I get excited over that when Jesus promised me 100-fold?

We have a God who loves us.

I pour everything I have into people because people are God's number one investment. Jesus said to Peter, "Feed My sheep." (Read John 21:15-17.)

When I see what I am willing to do for people, I think about how much more God can and will do. He said, "If ye then, being evil, know how to give good gifts unto your children, how much more shall your Father which is in Heaven give good things to them that ask Him?" (Matthew 7:11).

God is looking for Receivers.

There is a little girl that I love very much. I have known her since she was a year-and-a-half old. About every 3 or 4 weeks she will text me, "Where are you? I miss you. I want to see you. I want to spend some time with you." I am like a father to her. She loves pink so I bought her a pink TV. I have bought her an iPad with a pink wraparound case, a pink iPhone, even pink luggage; because that is what she likes.

She always responds, "How did you know this is just what I wanted?" She is the best Receiver I have ever met in 65 years. God wants to find us as Receivers.

Pray these words. "Lord, I receive Your nature. Lord, I receive Your love. I receive Your Prosperity. I receive Your Assignment in my life. I am a Receiver. Thank You, Lord for Your promises to me."

What Are 4 Things You Should Do Tomorrow?

Meet with The Holy Spirit for 7 minutes every morning and introduce your financial needs to Him. Say, "Teach me Your financial Laws."

You should put up pictures of your goals and your dreams around your house where you can see the things that you want.

Go to whoever is involved in your finances, your boss or anyone else and say, "Would you teach me?" If you know anybody's got money, ask them to teach you. Say, "Would you give me Step 1, Step 2? What should I be doing?"

Invest in books and CDs. Go to bookstores like Barnes & Noble. There are people who are worth billions who have documented their discoveries.

Decide you are going to learn something every day. Decide to be a learner.

Get a picture of who you want to help. Who do you want to bless? What do you want to accomplish with your life? There are only so many clothes you can buy, or so much you can spend on a car. You can take care of yourself pretty quick. It does not take a whole lot to take care of yourself.

The More Important People Become To You, The More Important Your Money Will Become To You.

When you see people you want to bless, to help, to encourage and things you want to accomplish; that will require money.

I remember when a 76-year-old widow came up to me crying because she was being kicked out of her house. She had lived in the house for 16 years and was carrying a note. I told her, "I will get you a lawyer. We will pay for it and you will keep your house."

According to Ephesians 6:8, *What You Make Happen For Others, God Will Make Happen For You.* I do not follow my gift through the door. Deceitful men use gifts to control others.

As men and women of God who love God, we sow because God has been good to us.

Say these words, "I am a Receiver. I am a Receiver of Divine Knowledge. I am a Receiver of Favor. In Jesus' Name."

Favor Must Become Your Seed Before It Becomes Your Harvest. Lavish Favor into your world.

What You Make Happen For Others, God Will Make Happen For You.

If you cannot trust God with your money, why do you think you are going to end up all right in Heaven? If you cannot believe Him in Luke 6:38, 2 Corinthians 9:6, Mark 10:28-30 and Malachi 3:8-10; why can you believe John 3:16?

Find your inspiration. If you can find what inspires you, you cannot fail. I did not understand this until the last two and one-half years when I had the roughest years of my life.

About 6 months ago, I began to get restored, but two years ago in the month of July, I plummeted emotionally and mentally; the lowest level I have ever been in my lifetime. I lost all inspiration for anything. I was demoralized and unspeakably disappointed in people, and I was stunned to look at people that I had invested in and saw no reward, saw no fruit, saw no Harvest, and it messed my head up.

I did not want to live. I hated everything I had ever done, every book I had ever written. That went on for months, and the Lord began to work with my life, and show me how to get my focus back on what inspired me; not who depressed me, but on what inspired me.

Find something that inspires you. It could be a song. You know that Rocky song, *Eye of the Tiger?* I always play that in my gym at my house. I can picture Rocky running. In my theater room, I have a picture of Mohammed Ali standing over Sonny Lister. I have Clint Eastwood on my right wall...because in movies I always see myself as the hero.

Find what inspires you. A song. A sound. A rose. A color.

Find what inspires you and put it front of you. A motorcycle. A basketball. I keep footballs around my bedroom just to remember my football days to keep myself motivated.

Find what inspires you. This is your life. Put it in front of you. The day will come you will be more blessed than you have ever been.

Today Is The Poorest You Will Ever Be The Rest of Your Life.

You have been willing to receive from The Word of God. You have been willing to make God your Partner. Get into covenant with God. Everything you have came from Him.

Our Prayer Together:

"Father, we thank You right now for every partner who has watched...every friend. Thank You for my precious friend. They are Receivers. They love Your Word. They love Truth. They love Wisdom. This day will mark a turnaround in their financial Mind...their financial anointing.

"I ask You boldly like Moses said, 'I cannot do this work by myself.' You said, 'Find 70 men who value the anointing.' Everything You put on me, You will give to them. What You blessed me with, You will bless them with.

"Lord, I ask that my friend reading this book will experience the most profound testimony within 12 months. May they understand my heart and Your heart. May they understand Your nature and Your character. Wherever they work, or if they have not been able to really find the center of their Assignment; I ask You within 21 days from today to place them in the center of their Assignment.

"Reveal it through the path of Favor. Reveal it through the path of Opportunity. Reveal it through the presence of peace in their spirit. Everything You do for me, do for them.

"Lord, if You call me home, let this same grace and understanding that You put in my heart come up on them and may everything they touch be blessed, in Jesus' Name."

"I command The Blessing towards you that everything you touch because you treasure the Wisdom of God...everything that you touch will be blessed. I release you to lavish Favor in your environment. I release you to a life of receiving and a life of excellence, that every time you receive an instruction, you complete it with excellence.

"I decree that wherever you walk, a Financial Authority rest upon you and every environment you enter must submit to the Divine Assignment in your life.

"Every time God blesses me, may He bless you too. When God gives me a jet, He gives you one. When God gives me a Mercedes, He gives you one. I release you to the Wisdom of God, in Jesus' Name."

≈ 7 ≈

YOUR FUTURE IS DECIDED BY WHO YOU BELIEVE

Hidden Prejudices Keep Men Poor.

Too many people do not understand the character of God. Increase is part of the Divine nature within us.

Many people do not know this and suffer with hidden prejudices that have been planted over the years. The antidote is hearing His Voice through His Word and developing confidence in Him.

Our goals and our dreams are so vast, and so needy that we cannot be ashamed to be His financial partner in the world. We can only confront adversity freely, and quickly if we understand we are right to pursue Divine blessing. The mantle of Biblical Prosperity must matter to us more than the opinions of others.

When our world view is corrected, ministers whose dreams have been crushed and diminished because they simply did not have the finances to fulfill their Assignment will come back alive.

This book, *Why Men Stay Poor,* is being presented as a case for Prosperity. We must deal with any hypocrisy that has crept into the crevices of our philosophy. We need the help of The Holy Spirit to see the contradiction involved in those who seem to be anti-

Prosperity but want the boss to give them a raise. My goal is to deal strongly with these things.

I know the *power* of a thought.

I know the *influence* of a righteous thought.

I know the *competence* of correct thinking.

Truth is a demolisher of error. There are so many falsehoods on earth. Falsehood is the only way you can be tricked. The only way that you can be deceived is through receiving wrong information or wrong counsel.

I have mentioned several times that I have two supreme fears within me.

1. The Fear of Believing A Lie. I fear embracing a philosophy, or even a warped principle, that has been abused or misused. I have an unexplainable obsession for Divine truth. That is why the Bible is so important to me.

A young preacher said to me, "Dr. Murdock, I have noticed out of all the books that you write, you also publish Bibles. You published a Bible just for teenagers. You published another Topical Bible just for children that is built around the topics that concern them. You published one for mothers, one for fathers, one for businesswomen, and another for businessmen."

My answer to him was simple, "This traces back to my fear of being deceived and having a burning desire to keep others from deception."

I have one called *The Survival Bible.* When your life is in a crisis, it contains what to read in the Bible. I have nothing else I believe in the earth except God. Believing people leads to disappointment, because of liars and deceivers.

Thank God I discovered The Holy Spirit. I am so

thankful that I had a dad who was persuaded concerning the Bible. I never experienced a moment of his doubts. It is marvelous to live in an environment for your first 18 years of life being persuaded that the presence of God heals, restores.

2.   I Fear Insufficiently Expressing Thankfulness. My second fear is not expressing my thankfulness *effectively.* I really battle against unthankfulness in my life, because it was the first sin. It was the sin that entered Heaven.

Unthankfulness is probably the only sin that entered the Presence of God. Lucifer, was an archangel, chief of all the angels. He was the most beautiful creature God had ever created, but He was unthankful for the gift of access. He was unthankful for his difference. He was unthankful for the gift of God within him.

What is Prosperity? *Prosperity Is Having Enough Provision To Complete A Divine Instruction.* Prosperity is having enough money to fulfill an Assignment from The Holy Spirit. Prosperity is having enough Favor, health, money, energy and passion to *complete* your Assignment, and *fulfill* the expectations of God toward us.

Do I need help? *Absolutely.*

Do I need Favor with people and God? *Of course.*

Do I need open doors? Do I need partnership with my life so I can do the commands of God? *You bet your life I do.*

Do I need money? *Yes.*

If I want to help anybody on the earth at any level, if I want to send someone to Bible College. If I want to print a book. If I want to build a church. If I want to buy a car. I need money.

I leave for Nigeria next week. The ticket cost is horrendous. I need money if I want to do good on the earth.

Is it Scriptural to discuss money? I believe so.

Twenty percent of what Christ talked about was money. Twenty percent of His parables, His teachings, regarded riches and Prosperity. Sometimes He discussed it from the standpoint of warning that we must be careful not to let it make us prideful, lose our humility, and stop depending on God.

Scripture talks about it being easier for a camel to go through a needle point than for a rich man to go to Heaven. That bothered me until Thomas Harrison, my Professor from Southwestern Assemblies of God Bible College explained it to us in class.

The gate into Jerusalem was often called *The Eye of The Needle*. It was a very narrow gate that was usually used by night visitors to Jerusalem. The narrowness of the gate required the fully-loaded camels to kneel and scoot their way through the gate. The camel could not walk in its usual manner, tall and proud.

Then I understood it is easier for a camel to go through the eye of a needle. It meant that there had to be superb humility. It means a breaking down of our pride.

Should religion get involved with money? Of all the organizations of the earth, religion should be consumed with understanding The Laws of Prosperity because our task requires so much of it.

We do not require money to build a casino, but we require money to purchase ships, airplanes, printing presses, radio stations, and TV stations. The Bible says that a man is worse than an infidel that does not provide for his own family.

The Bible always references wealth from the context of its usefulness. It is represented as a sign of being a blessing. Money is described as the fruit of an integrous relationship. The Scriptures even call poverty the consequence of rebellion. "Poverty and shame shall be to him that refuseth instruction," (Proverbs 13:18).

"Mike, if I ask God to bless me financially, is that a Scriptural prayer?" *Without a doubt.*

"If I ask The Holy Spirit to show me how to spend money wisely is that a godly prayer?" *It is absolutely in agreement with God's Word.*

"If I ask The Holy Spirit to help me own my own home so my children can be raised in a safe neighborhood, would God be angry at me because I want more money?" No. In fact, He tells you ways of behavior that influence your financial returns on the earth.

One of the most effective chapters in the Bible is Psalm 112. It is glorious, and it has changed my life. It tells us, "Blessed is the man that feareth the Lord, that delighteth greatly in His commandments...wealth and riches shall be in his house."

God doubled Job's money when satan came against him. Some people believe Job's story about God taking away from him, but it wasn't God that took away from him. Job's false assessment of his tragedy was probably due to no Mentorship.

The oldest book in the Bible is the book of Job. It was recorded before Genesis. Job had no Bible. Job had no financial teaching, yet the Bible refers to him as a righteous man.

The King James Version of the Bible calls Job, "a perfect man." Job was so perfect that he attracted demonic attention. Satan appeared in the Presence of God and said, "Doth Job serve You for naught?" Does he serve You for nothing?

Satan was saying, "The reason Job serves you is he gets a benefit." If satan ever told the truth, that would be one time he did.

We Do Not Serve God Without Compensation.

There is a Divinely relentless, unfailing, unchanging, tangible Reward System in the Scriptures. I love it. I love Deuteronomy 28. I love Malachi 3. I love 2 Corinthians 9:6. I love Mark 10:28-30. I love Luke 6:38 where He gives us 7 levels of receiving from the Lord.

The Catholic Church has purchased billions of dollars of buildings and companies all over the world. They have done this through the nickels and dimes of millions of people who were broke. They were not taught to sow with expectation.

Many have been taught that we should only give because of the Greatness of God. Others are taught you should give because you owe a debt to God.

There is a whole history of the rich versus the poor throughout history. Why are men poor who work in a prosperous city? Why are men poor who go to church, open their Bible and read these Scriptures: "If ye then, being evil, know how to give good gifts unto your children, how much more shall your Father which is in Heaven give good things to them that ask Him?"

One place talks about giving The Holy Spirit to those that love Him. What about Psalm 84:11 that says, "No good thing will He withhold from them who walk uprightly."?

"Well Brother Mike, I am walking uprightly and I am broke."

Such a problem qualifies for your total scrutiny.

What is wrong with me that my car breaks down and the mechanic wants $1,200.00 and I only have $400.00 in my bank account?

I want to send my daughter to Bible School but she has no money. We have no money. We can't even buy a car. We cannot pay the tuition, and if you want to know a costly education, try going to a private Christian school. Almost no Christian can afford the cost of a Christian school.

How dare we battle against the teaching of Prosperity? Either you are a fool or you are a bona fide 24-karat hypocrite! How dare we raise our voice against financial blessing? How dare we position ourselves against the anointing of God upon men and women to release Prosperity into The Kingdom of God? How dare we raise our voice when our taxes run up to 40 percent of our income?

Why would you be upset when you give God the 10 percent, the little dime He asks for when Washington, D.C., and the Internal Revenue Service requires up to 40 percent of your income? Here in America you only get to keep about half of what you make.

Then you go to a store with the half you have left

and they add 8 percent onto your sale. You go to
another store in another area and the tax rate is lower,
but it is still 6 percent. Eventually you say, "What on
earth is going on here? How will I survive? How will I
get by?"

Why Do Men Stay Poor? Is there a reason? Is it
God's responsibility to fill up my bank account?

There are two parts of the Gospel. *The Person of
Jesus Creates Your Peace. The Principles of Jesus,* what
He taught, *Decide Your Prosperity.*

No man serving God can expect God to make him
a millionaire simply because he gave his heart to Jesus.
Prayer does not guarantee Prosperity. Some of the most
effective prayer warriors in the prayer room have asked
me to pay their light bill, buy them a car, help them on
their gasoline, or pay for their apartment rent.

*Having a great Assignment does not guarantee
Prosperity.* I could not count the missionaries who have
begged me to raise support for them. Others ask, "Will
you please send us a monthly check?"

The Goodness of People Does Not Attract Money.
You may respond, "Really?" Some of the best people I
know can hardly survive.

"Well, Brother Mike, if God loves me He will give
me money."

The love of God does not affect your finances. That
was the most difficult understanding of my whole life.

Daddy is a great example of this truth. I think
most would believe that if I served God, read my Bible,
lifted my hands, and pioneered 7 churches, Prosperity
would flow.

Surely someone would have Financial Blessing by

building churches in Cameron, Louisiana, Sweet Lake, Louisiana, Big Lake, Louisiana, Lake Charles, Louisiana, and Franklin, Louisiana. Daddy started churches with nothing. He simply believed that God called him.

He had enough money to keep us fed. I would not say fed well. We did not have meat very often. I do not recall anytime in my 18 years of living at home when I had two slices of bologna on the same sandwich. This was even with Daddy constantly preaching and praying.

When Mother decided to work for K-Mart, about the year I decided to go to Bible college, we had some extra spending money. The most my father's church ever gave him as a salary was from the Calcasieu Tabernacle. There were some men with money on the church board, but year after year Daddy received his highest salary ever...$125.00 a week.

There was no extra money for his house. No extra money was provided for his car. There was no money given for gasoline. Month after month and year after year, not one time did they even offer him a raise, not for a decade.

In the meanwhile, I was reading the Bible and wondering why are there men with millions who do not even serve God, but have millions? I wondered, "Why are missionaries broke? They have left their homes. They have left their families. They have gone around the world."

In Nairobi, several missionaries challenged me in my teaching on Prosperity. I was in my 20's and they pleaded with me not to tell the Africans about

Prosperity.

They said, "Brother Mike, there is no money here in Africa."

I said, "You have 6 servants and you pay each one of them $1.00 a day." They paid their help $30.00 a month.

I remember Suzie. She was a wonderful young African lady. She had two little children, and they gave her a dollar a day.

I said to the missionaries, "If you are going to pay these people $1,000.00 a year to be your servant; work them 40 and 50 hours a week in exchange for enough money to buy a little rice, do not you think they should know about The Laws of Prosperity?"

They would argue. They would stop me on the roads while I was driving in Nairobi. They would pull me over and stuff through the window articles from *The Pentecostal Evangel*, the international magazine of The Assemblies of God Headquarters teaching against, "The Horrible Tragedy of The Prosperity Gospel."

It was difficult for me. It was very hard for me to handle. How can we be blessed and tell others the blessing is not for everybody? How can we tell them it is just for some people?

Why do men stay poor...*with a rich God?*

Why do men stay poor in a prosperous world of oil, silver, gold and diamonds? Why do people stay poor?

There is more than one reason. The reasons are many, not just one.

1. Many Poor People Have No Inspiration. Some people have been taught adaptation to poverty. Some people have been trained to live within a small amount of money. They have not been inspired by anybody to prosper.

Too many have been taught to submit, to adapt, and to accept. I admit that adaptation is a golden tool in any environment. Certainly adaptation was the key to Joseph's life when he adapted to the prison, but refused to accept it. He adapted and refused to be a complainer and retaliator. Then God honored and promoted him.

Everywhere the Bible talks about God blessing somebody, it is about money. The 100-fold return is mentioned. It is connected to Isaac's life. It is linked to Abraham's blessing.

The 112th Psalm, which is my theme Psalm for my life, is why I plant $112.00 Seed every Sunday of my life. On the first day of every week I automatically focus my $112.00 Seed into The Kingdom of God. Why do I do this? It is an expression of faith that I am in covenant with the 112th Psalm.

Who crushed your inspiration? Who broke you down? Who tore you apart?

2. Some Stay Poor Because They Have No Heroes. Their heroes are poor people who had nothing, and they wanted to be like them. Some people had no Mentorship. Nobody taught them.

My father privately expressed something profound to me after a service where I had taught. He said, "Son, you know I was raised on the farm...78 acres owned by my father, Ira T. Murdock in Grapeland, Texas."

Daddy made a statement that profoundly touched my heart. "I was raised on the farm. It never crossed our Mind not to expect a Harvest. Son, if somebody would have taught me and Mother what God has taught you about Prosperity, our entire ministry would have been different."

I Cannot Change Your Life Until I Change Who You Trust.

I Cannot Change Your World Until I Know Who You Honor.

Mentorship is the Seed for more...if it is accurate. Who taught you to expect little? It ruined your life for eternity. One lie can last 10 generations.

3. Some People Stay Poor Because They Set No Goals. Having no goals limits your vision that unlocks your faith. It is your vision that gives you endurance power. It is your goal that takes you up and over the hurdles of life.

Create a dream wall. Somewhere there should be a wall full of pictures of the Tomorrow you intend to produce. If you want to own an airplane, put a picture of a jet on your wall.

If you want to go to a college, put a picture of a certificate on that wall. Turn your Mind inside out until everything you want to experience is on your wall.

Harvard University did a 10 year study and they found out 3 percent of a particular graduating class of Harvard had made more money than the other 97 percent who graduated that same year.

They studied the lives of the graduating class for one solid year. They concluded that 3 percent of the graduating class had made more money, had more land, had more finances, than the other 97 percent combined.

Their intensive study that lasted over a year found only one difference. The 97 percent had never written down a list of their financial goals. Only 3 percent of the graduating class had ever written down a list of their financial goals.

4. Some People Stay Poor Because They Are Prejudiced Against The Rich. They resent them. They retaliate. They envy.

It is impossible to learn from somebody you resent. You can only learn from somebody you admire. Some people are prejudiced against the rich because they have had bad experiences.

Gratitude Is The Seed For Multiplication. Ingratitude is a major ingredient in poverty. *Whatever You Are Thankful For Will Multiply In Your Life.*

5. Some People Stay Poor Because They Continuously Lose Favor, And Favor Is The Seed For Blessing.

Everywhere There Is Honor There Is Favor.

Everywhere There Is Favor There Is Money.

Honor *attracts* money. Show me where you have dishonored someone or something, and I will show you a closed door.

6. Some Stay Poor Because They Dishonor Authority. Money flows down, not up. Somebody authorized to give you instructions is authorized to *promote* you.

The 10 Commandments are about Honor. The first 4 are about Honoring God. The next 6 are about Honoring people. The first commandment of the 10 with a promise of Reward System is number 5, "If I Honor my Mother and Father, it will go well with me."

7. Some People Stay Poor Because They Never Develop An Interest In Productivity. The

Bible says God will reward every man according to his work. *Some people casualize their money.* They never learn how to turn a dollar into 5. They do not learn how to turn a $10.00 bill into $200.00.

Some never negotiate. Some sow in wrong soil.

I am going to make an offer to you that I think is going to be an incredible blessing to you. I am going to ask you in the next 3 days to plant $112.00 Seed as a Financial Covenant with God. I am going to ask you to sow your first Seed in the next 72 hours, $112.00 Seed.

I am going to ask you to focus that Seed for one thing and that is for *112 days of Financial Favor* on the earth. I want every person to do this. I am not ashamed of being a multimillionaire. I am not embarrassed at that.

I have known what it meant to lose money in oil. I have lost money everywhere you can use it except in one way and that is in my Covenant with God. My Covenant with God. I am in Covenant with the Wealth Giver of the Universe.

I am talking about 112 days of Financial Favor. All it takes is for somebody to like you. All it takes is somebody to like you.

I started to bless some people in the last 24 hours, I came so close to blessing some people with some hundred dollar bills and The Holy Spirit stopped me. I knew why within hours.

I want to tell you there are people ready to bless you. There are people ready to open the door for you but you have got to please God.

I broke the back of poverty with a $1,000.00 Seed. I was 36 years old. I did not own a kitchen table. I had no chairs to sit on in my house. I had just moved from California. I will not tell you how broke I was except to tell you I could not buy a kitchen chair. I could not buy a table.

A royalty check came in for me, $5,000.00 from ASCAP, American Society of Composers And Publishers. I went to help a preacher on his TV program, and he looked into the screen and told everybody to plant a $1,000.00 Seed.

That was on a Wednesday morning. God told me to do it two more times, from Wednesday morning to Sunday. God spoke to me to plant three $1,000.00 Seeds.

On Sunday night a man walked up who is wealthy here in Dallas. He said, "I have a very rare automobile. There are only 19 of them in the world. God told me to give it to you." And that launched a very successful...I started to say season, but it has been years.

I broke the back of poverty with a $1,000.00 Seed. Everywhere I preach people come up to me all over the world and say, "Because of you God made me a millionaire."

I got up one morning in church and said, "If you never do it again, I want you to plant a $112.00 Seed and put your check on top of the 112th Psalm and see what God will do."

My sister, Flo, wrote down a list of 8 Miracles she had never asked God for in her lifetime. On the following Friday she came over to my house next door, I live next door to her. She sat there watching me and she said, "Mike, this $112.00 Seed really works, doesn't it?"

I said, "Did you do that Sis?"

She said, "I did."

I said, "Did anything happen?"

She said, "Every one of my list of 8 Miracles happened. Not even a week is over."

I looked at her from my recliner and I said, "Sis, if people knew about the $112.00 Seed, what I know about the 112th Psalm, they would sell furniture to get $112.00. They would sell their table. They would sell their recliner. They would sell what they have in their house to get it, if they could see what I see in it."

As you are reading this I urge you to set aside a Seed of $112.00.

If you sneer at this and you casualize it and you say, "Well, I do not know if that will work for me." If that is the way you feel about the God you serve, do not sow it. *Don't you sow one Seed if you do not trust the character of God.* But do not ever forget I gave you the instruction.

Some preachers came up to me after a conference and said, "Brother Murdock, we do not feel like you should be telling everybody about all your blessings."

I said, "What has made you think I told them all? I have not told a human in my life all the blessings."

I believe in Miracles because I believe in God. I believe that mountains can be moved because I believe in God. Nothing is impossible. I have decided to believe in God. I believe in Miracles.

"Lord, I ask You to give them 112 days of the supernatural for Your glory. So be it. In Jesus' Name." Glory to God.

I want you to write in your Bible today: 112 Days

of Financial Favor. You are going to be amazed.

There is something so spectacular that is going to happen. There is somebody right now about to sow an Uncommon Seed and your Harvest is going to start within 72 hours. There is something electrifying about this Seed.

If what I am teaching you is Biblical, Scriptural and of God, I Covenant that the next 112 days of your world will be a relentless unending diary. *A journal of Financial Favor*...112 Days of Financial Favor.

You are going to attract it like a magnet from the north, from the south, from the east, from the west. You are going to look back at this little $112.00 Seed and you are going to be like me and say, "I have got to do this every week. I have got to do this every Sunday."

Watch what God will do. Document your Harvest.

I will never forget the day God spoke to my heart about a person, and she is a daughter in the Lord, but God spoke to my heart to bless her and Honor her and buy a most beautiful Mercedes. God stirred my heart to plant that as a Seed into her life.

You do not need but one person liking you. You do not need a whole world. You just need one person believing that you are for real. One person believing you are quality soil.

I had a man come up and give me the most gorgeous ring. I was in a Partner meeting. I just stopped overnight on my way back home. He walks up to me in the front, takes off his most gorgeous ring, pulls it off his hand. I said, "I do not wear many rings." He said, "God told me to give this to you." I put it on my finger and I felt like one of those rich men, you know. It just takes one person to believe in you.

Why won't you trust the character of God? What is wrong with you? Why would you hold on to $1,000.00 when your dream is 100 times that? Why would you hold on to $1,000.00?

I have felt there is going to be a phenomenal unprecedented Financial Authority come on my own life. I want my financial secretary to write two Seeds today. One $112.00 for 112 Days of Financial Favor, and write one for $1,000.00 for the Rebekah Home. That is a Home for unwed mothers that we are raising support for.

"Father, Your sheep know Your voice and another will not follow. I trust You. I trust Your Voice. Every person has been given an Assignment.

"Father, there is somebody so broke, they are so backwards in their finances, they do not even have $112.00. Today they will step out in faith and say, 'By Faith I will sow this.' In Jesus' Name Honor them for it." Praise God.

We are going to break the back of Poverty. Hallelujah.

Goliath Is The Door To Every New Season. Until you have a Goliath in your life, you are still in the pasture. Get excited when you have an adversary.

8

DECISIONS DECIDE WEALTH

Knowledge of Financial Laws Decide Wealth.

"Precious Holy Spirit, I praise You tonight for the access that You have given us to Your Word, to Your Principles, to Your Laws, especially Your Presence. Let this book be truly stress removing, inspiring us to succeed in every part of our lives, especially in our financial world.

"Lord, You have placed this subject so strong on my heart, *Why Men Stay Poor.* Use it to wipe out debt. Use our time together as a strategic sword killing the financial stress that multiplies in our family and within our home.

"We love Your Law. We love the World-Class desires that You have for us. We love that Father. We are anointed to receive Uncommon Wisdom. You placed this on my heart.

"Father, You give every man a message from this page. Our pain is a birthplace for our Assignment. What we hate we can conquer. Where we hurt the most we receive revelation.

"We know there are many parts of our life such as physical disease and sickness, relationships, restoration, self-confidence, but in the problem zone with finances we find answers through Your Word and we love that. We love that. Amen." Praise God.

I can't say enough gratitude to the Lord for placing this on my heart, because what I teach is so foreign to the beginning environment of my life; environment of my early ministry. This is why it is so important.

Most of us have been taught adaptation to lack...to build our lives around small things.

Many of us have been trained to anticipate a spectacular Heaven with gold streets, angelic wings fluttering, a long banquet table for a few million of us, but few of us have been trained to find the hidden gold that is close to us on the earth.

I had a man tell me one time, "I do not like this silver and gold and diamond stuff."

I laughingly replied, "Take that up with God when we arrive in Heaven. Tell God that you have little respect for the stones that He placed on the earth that have value, that can be used as currency."

I have mentioned a number of things in our beginning. One is, "Should religion be involved in money? Should it be involved in the teaching of it?"

Isn't that a world subject like golf, tennis and soccer?

Should Christians even have an interest in money?

I would say at any level you should be interested in finances.

I am going to encourage you to invest in Financial Knowledge and Mentorship. One of the best books I have found for millionaires to be is a book called, *Acres of Diamonds* by Russell Conwell, the Baptist Preacher who birthed Temple University. He lectured on this topic around the world.

Another book is *The Millionaire Next Door.*

The two best books that I have written on finances, are...one is called, *Secrets of The Richest Man Who Ever Lived.* My 19-year research on King Solomon. Then the book Benny Hinn requested I write for his Partners entitled, *31 Reasons People Do Not Receive Their Financial Harvest.* Both are spectacular. Both are life-changing. Both will save you hundreds of thousands of dollars.

We have talked about the necessity of Financial Inspiration.

Passion is a birthplace.

Passion is a Seed for energy, research, learning.

Isaiah 1:17 has electrified my heart on more than one occasion...*Learn to do well.*

God did not say, "Pray to do well." Because *Wisdom Is The Ability To Recognize Difference, Difference Between Divine Responsibility And Human Responsibility.*

It is not God's responsibility to paralyze a thief trying to enter your house. It is your responsibility to *lock* the door.

It is not God's responsibility to smite the man who enters your daughter's bedroom. It is your responsibility to reach for your gun and give him a memorable experience.

I am a strong believer in identifying the difference between God's responsibility and mine.

Somebody needs to light your fire. Somebody needs to unleash your imagination for Tomorrow. Somebody needs to expose any area, any falsehood that has entered your life from childhood.

Many people believe that God decides who has

money and who does not.

If God is the decision-maker of the flow of Wealth, explain why missionaries are broke and evil men are billionaires.

Decisions Decide Wealth.

Knowledge of Financial Laws decide wealth.

The ability to build and maintain worthwhile relationships is a part of wealth.

Negotiation for everything you buy is a part of Wealth.

You need inspiration. What excites you to produce? What wakes up the energy within you? Do you have a dream wall at your house with pictures of your dreams, your goals, your Tomorrow? If I walked into your home what is the conversation I receive from the walls of your house?

I was noticing a picture the other day. I really love Spanish style buildings. I love flat roof homes. I love Spanish tile, the orange or the deep clay red. I love what I love. I move toward what I love and I put what I love in front of me so that what I hate cannot dominate my Mind. If you win in your Mind, you win in your finances.

The financial battle is not at the bank. The financial battle of life is in your Mind. What do I desire?

Desire makes you *creative.*

Desire makes you *powerful and strong.*

Desire makes you *capable of withstanding adversity.*

Desire makes you *discerning.*

Whatever you desire in life, something you want to become, something you want to do, something you want to have, that desire is a magnet for knowledge.

When I look at something that excites me, the path to it becomes clear, easy to understand.

One of my Wisdom Keys says, *When The Heart Decides The Destination, The Mind Designs A Map To Reach It.*

Who inspires you?

Did you know I never liked the word 'inspiration' until maybe two years ago. I never liked that word, it seemed too milky. It seemed shallow.

I would see signs...things to inspire you. I hated that word 'inspire.' My specific word for it is 'motivate.' What motivates you? *Motivate means reason for doing something.* What is my motivation?

Did you hear the General last night talk about ISIS and how they would break them down in 3 hours? They first had to know their motivation, and number two their greatest fear. What was their greatest motivation and what was their greatest fear? That enabled them to extract life-saving knowledge concerning terrorist attacks, bombs and plans.

You have to be inspired.

I love the words of Aristotle Onassis, the Greek tycoon who married Jacqueline Kennedy, the widow of President John F. Kennedy, he said, "If it wasn't for women, men would not even have a need for money." He referenced that men want to do things for the women in their life...the Princess that has touched and ignited their heart.

There is nothing on earth as exciting as a woman. It was God's final creation of a huge universe. God had practiced on everything and then He made woman...the highest Crown of His creation.

In Proverbs 31 we see it easily and quickly that it is the woman who is the Wealth Manager of her house. The man can create streams of Honor, finances, but the woman, according to Genesis and the search of Abraham's chief steward Eleazar for the Wealth Manager of Isaac's wealth and Abraham's wealth, was in the woman he would select to walk beside him.

Many women are skilled at spending it. But not spending it wisely. That was the difference in the Proverbs 31 woman.

Why do men stay poor in a prosperous earth? Why do men stay impoverished when they were created by a wealthy, rich God?

One Is Their Prejudice Against The Rich. A bad experience against someone wealthy, so they grow up thinking, how do they get their wealth?

Even our politician's think that the wealthy get the money from the poor. There are actually people who believe that men's wealth came from impoverishing other men.

Then you study the life of Sam Walton who died worth $5 billion and left each of his children $1 billion a piece. You found out not only did he become wealthy, but he is the number one employer on the earth. Wal-Mart has employed more people who bring money home to their families than any other business we know of.

We have learned about the importance of relation-ships because money begins inside you. I am not talking about a dollar bill in your pocket. I am talking about anything that is worth something. *Money is anything of exchangeable value.*

Some months ago, The Holy Spirit kept giving me a sentence from the Scriptures about treasures in dark places...I pondered on that. I understood that the earth's soil contains billions and billions and billions. There is the oil underneath the dirt, underneath the soil is the stream of oil.

Under the soil is gold and silver and diamonds and coal. I talked about the stones of jade. I talked about all the wealth of the earth and how we are walking on wealth every day of our life.

The Holy Spirit is a Master Financial Adviser. If you will accept His voice as irreplaceable, He will talk to you *more* than anyone has talked to you. If you *ask* Him questions, He will *answer.* If you *depend* on His counsel, He will be relentless in *revealing* strategies, ideas, valuable relationships.

Everything God wants to give you is hidden in a human. Love is the Seed for discovering Divine wealth. Genius is hidden in every human. Discovering your own is a gate to your Future.

Everything should be negotiated. I like what one well-known negotiation seminar says: "You do not get in life what you deserve, you get what you negotiate for."

I walked into a luggage store at Las Colinas, a community outside of Dallas, in Irving, Texas. I said to the lady, "I would like a corporate discount."

She said, "I never heard of that, what is that?"

I said, "It is 40 percent off."

The bookstores buy books from distributors at 60 to 70 percent off. The distributors who sell it to the bookstores and the bookstores get a 40 percent discount; some negotiate 50 percent. You can only be told no.

I like to walk into places and say, "What do you

have on sale for a poor man?" So they will know I am money-conscious. I want every man that does business with me to know that I will study his price and get 6 more to compare it with. I want them to know. I am collecting because I am negotiating.

Remember that Jesus cursed every man who did not multiply. *Multiplication is a command.* God expected us to multiply.

Jesus had the opposite teaching of Washington, D. C., who say, "Strip the man who has 5 talents and give his talents over here to a man with one." But in the Scriptures the man who refused to use his one talent, was stripped and his talent was given to the man with 5. *Success breeds success.*

Presentation Is The Seed For Acceptance.

Whether it is a woman presenting herself to a man like Esther, or Abigail presenting herself to David, or the woman with two coins, small pennies presenting her Offering to God, or Solomon killing 1,000 sheep, presenting them to God.

Presentation is so vital God invested His own Son on a cross so that the presentation would never be forgotten, and to this day the presentation infuriates evil hearts of evil men.

Presentation is for impact.

Negotiate. Do you know how to negotiate? Do you know the words to say? Let me give you an example. I had 4 bids to repair a roof on a house I had lived in for 30 years. Two were in the $7,000.00 bracket, one was in the $4,000.00 bracket. I went to the most expensive contractor I knew. I said, "I want you to come look at my roof."

I thought, man, he is going to charge me

$10,000.00. He always charges me more. But he was so smart he knew an inexpensive way to repair my roofs. He charged me something like $730.00. But the other 3 bids were for thousands of dollars.

There is a plumbing company in Haltom City. We asked for one, I think at the time we were getting 4-6 bids. Remember get 7 bids, get 5 bids. If you do not like them, get 5 more. If you do not like them, get 5 more.

Somebody has the equipment to do the job quickly, swiftly, more accurately, and the most deceitful phrase I have heard in my life is, "You get what you pay for." No, you do not. You never, never, never get what you pay for.

I have paid $40.00 for a plate of food I hated. I have paid $5.00 for a plate of food I love. No, you do not get what you pay for. *The price never indicates the quality.* Men who want to charge you a lot of money for things will tell you that.

Challenge what you hear. Test what you hear. Truth is *fearless* under scrutiny. In fact, truth knows that scrutiny brings confirmation.

If I recall, one company bid $76,000.00 to do the plumbing at my father's house. We found another plumber to do it for $7,000.00. *Negotiate everything.*

1. Men Stay Poor Because They Will Not Challenge The Prices In Their World.

2. Men Stay Poor Because They Do Not Know How To Talk Upward. They know how to scream at their kids but they do not know how to talk to Authority. *Authority is the source of Prosperity.* It is not someone under you that makes you prosperous. It is someone over you that makes you prosperous from the 5th commandment to the 10th.

3.   Men Stay Poor Because They Do Not Know How To Birth Favorable Circumstances.

4.   Men Stay Poor Because They Are Unproductive. The Bible says God will reward every man according to his work.

One man came to me a number of years ago and said, "I want a raise."

I said, "I do too. Why should I give you a raise?"

"Well, I am buying a car and it is going to cost me a lot of money."

I had a secretary say the same thing. I landed in the airplane, she handed me a note, said, "I would like to make $1,000.00 more a month."

I said, "All of us would. Now why should I pay you $1,000.00 more?"

You know what she said? "Because me and my husband bought a new house and it is going to cost us $1,000.00 a month more than what we planned."

I said, "I pay you based on the problems you solve."

Your salary is based on the kinds of problems you have chosen to solve. It is not based on your age. It is not based on your likability. Every problem has *financial* value. That is why problems are so important on the earth. That is why until somebody has a problem, you are unnecessary. *You are as necessary as the problem you are solving.*

Today I sat in the passport office and the lady was explaining the 6 or 7 shots she was about to give me in the arm and how often some shots were needed. She was so smart. I was so gullible, so teachable I believed everything she said. I did not know anything different. She said it is all recorded right here.

I carry with me a *Live Scribe*. It is a notebook with

a pen, and the pen has a recorder in it. You document. Your notes are like tables of contents. If somebody starts talking to you write their name down, everything they say from there on...you can always go back and tap their name and hear everything they said. It is a fabulous tool for gathering information.

Knowledge is the Seed for wealth. My people are destroyed for lack of knowledge. Remember that the commands of Jesus were ask, seek, knock. *Everything you have not sought, you are lacking.*

As she began to talk I turned on my little recorder, another of my team members turned on her recorder and we began to record. Why? *Knowledge That Is Not Retrievable Is Not Usable.*

Now this lady was methodical. Probably well-paid because of the problems she solved. She sold us things that I would need. Everything from insect repellant...I bought it all. Why? I want to be well. I do not want to go to Nigeria and eat grapes when I should be taking off the peel of a banana and eating it instead. All of those things matter.

5. Men Stay Poor Because They Do Not Know What To Learn About. They do not learn about themselves because they do not know their gift.

6. Men Stay Poor Because They Do Not Ask Questions. The questions you ask decide what you discover.

I am not a rich man. I am not a wealthy man but I am a blessed man. I am a multimillionaire. I say that without hesitation but I am not a rich man. I do not consider a million dollars to be wealth at any level. It is when you are making $9.00 a hour. A million sounds like a lot, but not if you have billionaire desires.

Prosperous men ask questions poor men refuse to ask. Prosperous men build relationships with prosperous men.

Lost Favor is a quick road to poverty. What builds Favor? Honor? Problem-solving?

What are your greatest gifts from God? Are you a master listener? Are you a great conversationalist? Are you good at numbers? Are people comfortable around you? Are you good at technology?

What problems do you love to solve...dream of solving? Who do you admire...what are their problem-solving abilities? Who are you willing to learn from?

What are the last 3 questions you have asked your boss? What do you need to change that you are unwilling to change? What are you willing to stop doing?

If you are doing something for $10.00 an hour, what are you willing to start doing for $15.00 an hour?

I can teach anybody on my staff how to be worth $100,000.00. They have to be worth $40,000.00 first. They can't be worth $40,000.00 until they learn to be worth $20,000.00. If your boss has to tell you something twice, you qualify for half of your salary. If he has to tell you something the third time, now you are down to a third of your salary.

Do you know what agitates and what stops the flow and the river of Favor in your environment?

Do you create discomfort or comfort? How do you build credibility?

Who wants to do business with you? Who is willing to do business with you?

There is a book that is worth reading, *How To Swim With The Sharks Without Being Eaten.* Another is called, *Getting Things Done* by David Allen.

One of the wealthiest men I know reads every biography he can. He has read 7,000 since he gave his life to Christ.

Who are you learning from?

Whose books are you willing to read?

One sentence from Bill Gates (when he was worth $87,000,000,000.00) from a book he wrote changed my world. He said his dream was to have a *paperless* office. I could not imagine a paperless office so I asked somebody, "Explain what a computer is."

Nobody ever told me a computer is an information system where you can gather and retrieve knowledge within seconds and even distribute instructions within minutes. I knew nothing about Google. I knew nothing about Ask.com. I knew nothing about Apple. I knew nothing about Android systems or IOS systems. All I knew was that I had a hunger for knowledge. Where do I find it? How do I get it?

It never dawned on me that somebody can take a picture of things in a store and in seconds I can look at it and give them an instruction about the problem. I never understood opinions and consulting people's experiences on the Internet.

Seven years I asked for a website before I insisted on it. Seven years I asked everyone around me how to establish a website until I decided I would not live without one. *Life is whatever you are unwilling to live without.*

7. Men Stay Poor Because They Sow In Bad Soil Expecting A Harvest.

8. Men Stay Poor Because They Do Not Embrace The Character of God Described In

Scriptures.

9. Men Stay Poor Because They Never Learn To Walk Among Snakes. Jesus said we were to be as wise as serpents, yet appear as harmless as a dove.

10. Men Stay Poor Because They Exhaust Their Energy On Unworthy Battles.

11. Men Stay Poor Because They Casualize Money. They will fall to the concrete sidewalk to pick up a nickel, but they will not spend 5 minutes with their boss becoming their protégé.

12. Men Stay Poor Because They Refuse To Build A Reputation As A Problem-Solver.

13. Men Stay Poor Because They Dishonor Authority And Even Divine Laws.

14. Men Stay Poor Because They Refuse To Learn From Painful Mentors.

15. Men Stay Poor Because They Will Not Do Business With God.

16. Men Stay Poor Because They Do Not Develop Expectations of A Divine Harvest. Many expect their Harvest from men, instead of God. They think man is their source. God is your source. *God uses men, but my expectation is in God.*

You can sow your way out of trouble when God gives you instructions.

✎ 9 ✎

YOUR FOCUS DECIDES YOUR SUCCESS

"Father, You Are An Abundant God.

"You are a good God. You are a prayer answering God. You are a World-Class Listener to us. We love Your voice. We love Your words. We are adamant in keeping our ear next to Your mouth that every word You speak is never forgotten. Never. Never.

"Father, I thank You for this golden opportunity to pour truth into a chaotic world. To plant the Seed of order where there is tragic loss. To enter where love is absent, and be the volcano of victory that erupts. We are fearless toward the Future, thankful for Today. Master learners from the Past.

"Thank You, Father. Thank You. Thank You from the depths of my heart for Partners who believe what I believe: That the Bible is the answer for a broken generation. Your ship never gets capsized, and we are in Your ship. You are our Captain. We trust You with all of our hearts. Thank You, Father. Amen."

I am thrilled over what God puts in my heart, and even more thrilled that He has given me the Honor and the privilege of teaching part of His family on the earth while I am alive and that everything I say can improve your world...improve your life...correct your focus.

Wherever You Focus You Will Succeed.

Focus galvanizes invisible gifts within you: attentiveness, listening, Mind thoughts, energy.

1.   Some Men Stay Poor Because They Do Not Hate Poverty.

I plead with our pastors throughout the world to take a little time away from preaching on the Middle East and help us to create a money flow into our homes.

I do not have the ammunition and the guns Israel needs. I do not have them. There is not a cotton pickin' thing I can do about Hamas coming against Israel, but teach me how to have a prosperous home.

If you list your top 10 problems in your life right now, 9 out of 10 of them could be *resolved* with more money. "Well, money is not everything." *Money creates almost everything.*

Get off the hypocritical Phariseeism. I beg preachers everywhere to please tell the people about the God Who supplies; the God Who is a Gift Giver. The God Who is a covenant God.

I am so serious about finances. I am not desperate. I am not starving. My house is paid for. I am not trying to get anybody to pay for my house or buy me a car. I am trying to get you to wake up to doing business with God.

You can live a lifetime with an error. You never discover truths until you can't get something you want, and then you start looking into your belief system. Your belief system has sculptured your world...your philosophy.

I am not talking about surviving through the Salvation Army soup line. I am not talking about getting clothes for free on Tuesday at the local Good Will Store. I am discussing your *personal* world.

Success Is The Obtaining of A Worthwhile Goal.

2.   Some Men Stay Poor Because They Have Never Defined Success To Themselves.

Success has to be personalized. Success is very seasonal because your needs will change.

There was a time in my life where Success to me was having invitations to go preach and when somebody wanted me to go preach, I was successful. Now Success to me is the ability to stay home and focus on The Wisdom Center and write books instead of traveling everywhere.

What is your present definition of Success? Right now mine is finding a livable home near The Wisdom Center that has the unique quality of privacy. That is what I am looking for. That is why I have spent days looking at houses so that I do not have to drive past 10,000 cars to get to The Wisdom Center. That is my present definition; that is my next Success for me.

Yes, I am writing this book, finishing it up tonight...called *Why Men Stay Poor*. I have a house that is paid for, more than one, but I need a house that has the uniqueness of privacy because distraction is death to your Assignment. You have to sculpture an environment. In my scenario, I sculpture an environment where I can focus. That is my next personal success.

What is Success to you right now? Who is an *example?* Who *inspires* you? Who is in covenant with you for your present definition of Success? Your present definition may be from God. It may be out of your present inspiration.

Pain is usually the birthplace for a new goal.

I was thinking of the last time I was rushed to the Emergency Room, I made a little covenant I was going to start running every day and I am still not doing it.

So I am telling myself, you have to take care of your body. It takes more than pills to take care of your body. It takes more than a Bible under your arm to take care of your body. A Bible under my arm does not remove my waistline. So I began to think, what is Success to me? *What is Success now to me?* How do I want my life to be next? What do I want to become next?

3. Men Stay Poor When They Do Not Know The Divine Assignment Within Them.

4. Men Stay Poor When They Have Never Discovered The Divine Gift That Makes Them Unique Among Others.

5. Men Stay Poor Because They Are Unwilling To Learn From An Unhappy Person.

6. Men Stay Poor Because They Have Never Discerned The Hidden Gold In Those Around Them.

7. Men Stay Poor Because Their Mouth Multiplies Their Unbelief And Their Doubt.

8. Men Stay Poor Because They Refuse To Negotiate And Make Their Money More Important.

9. Men Stay Poor Because They Will Not Enter Into A Covenant With God.

10. Men Stay Poor Because They Will Not Find A Hero That Keeps Them Motivated.

11. Men Stay Poor Because They Have Become Distracted From Their Financial Goals.

12. Men Stay Poor Because They Let A Bad Experience Break A Relationship With Their Mentors.

13. Men Stay Poor Because of Ingratitude For Their Present.

14. Men Stay Poor Because They Dishonor Authority...The Only Source of Promotion.

God did not come down and get Joseph out of prison. It was Pharaoh that called him forth. Listen to Joseph's conversation to him. Astounding.

Listen to the Apostle Paul talk to Agrippa, reaffirming that he knew his value.

Success Is The Obtaining of A Worthwhile Goal. I first heard that from Paul J. Meyer. That is really not my Wisdom Key. If it is ever listed in my books as that I usually would reference Paul J. Meyer, head of Success Motivation Institute, called SMI.

In my late teens I discovered that man. I spent a whole day in his organization. First time I had ever written out my goals. He was the man that inspired me to write out my goals.

Then there is Claude Bristol who wrote the book *The Magic of Believing* and David Schwartz who wrote the book *The Magic of Thinking Big.*

Then there was Napoleon Hill who was worth knowing. He was given 100 letters to travel around the world and meet the wealthiest people on the earth. A man gave him a letter of introduction, but no money. Napoleon Hill wrote that book: *Think And Grow Rich.*

Think about your present opportunities. Think. Think about your difference from others. Think about sources of encouragement and your inspiration circle.

Hillary Clinton is one of the smartest women I

ever heard talk. I remember her statement in her book about it taking a village to raise a child. The criticism she attracted was ludicrous. It takes a church to grow a family. It takes a circle of people in your life to *unlock* the hidden treasures in you.

You Are A Walking Bank, Filled With Hidden Treasure. Somebody has a key to one. Somebody else has a key to another bank vault in you.

What is Success to you? How long will that be your present goal?

Success Is The Obtaining of A Worthwhile Goal.

15. Men Stay Poor Because They Do Not Ever Have A Real Picture of Their Future Success. They do not make a decision to have what they love instead of adapting to what they hate.

I made a statement to my staff. I had so many things that are problems that I finally just decided to solve all of them by calling in the blessing of the Lord. Look at your list. Your top 10 list of what you wish... let me give you an example.

We had to rush a young lady to the Emergency Room who had no medical insurance. "Well, I can't afford it," she said.

You see why you need medical insurance? Yes, it is expensive but you need it.

It is easier to call in the financial covenant with God than to try to live life without money.

You can adapt to any belief system you want.

God wants you to be productive. He said He will reward every man according to his work. I really do believe that.

What is Prosperity? Prosperity is having enough money to complete Divine expectations...having enough money to complete your Assignment on the earth.

Fathers, your family deserves a safe environment, so why attempt to *adapt* to an unsafe neighborhood?

What is your uniqueness? Is it marketed appropriately, properly, relentlessly? What kind of problem are you willing to solve for others?

The Problem You Solve Determines The Reward You Receive In Life.

A Problem Is A Golden Gate To Prosperity.

There is no Prosperity unless there is a problem. A problem is the reason there is Prosperity. Somebody solved a problem and is rewarded through the Scriptural system for it.

My job is not done when I finish telling you about Prosperity. My job is not done until you enter into a full persuasion that God is a worthy Business Partner. Do not withdraw from Him.

Think of what everybody does not know about you. Now think about what everybody does not know about God. Think about what is inside you that you have never seen. I have never seen my heart. I have never seen my blood vessels. There is so much in me I have never seen, but it is there.

Most of the world has never been seen by you. The greatest thoughts have never been thought by you. You know just enough to survive the day. Let God get involved. He is going to be the Smartest Person in your circle of counsel.

Fill up your walls with pictures of what excites you. If you can stay excited you can stay *creative.* If you stay creative you will never stay where you are. *Creativity Moves You From Your Present To Your Future.*

Your Future can begin 5 seconds from now. The

quality of it is inside your thoughts.

Get pictures of what you love. Put them in a notebook. Tear them out of magazines. Compile 100 to 150 pages of pictures that energize you: people, buildings, things, whatever excites you, a car, whatever gets your adrenalin going. Take it to Staples or an office supply store and have them to bind it in a black hard back book binder.

Find a way to put them on your phone. There is an app called Dropbox. It is like a lobby for the Internet world. Anything in the world you can put in a Dropbox. Dropbox is like a gate to the Internet world. I have thousands of transcripts in my Dropbox. I have pictures...it is called Spanish Inspiration because I love Spanish tile roofs.

I laughingly state if Heaven has no arches I am leaving. I love arches. Not the eyebrow arches, the full arches. I love orange colored tiles, Spanish tile. What do you love? What do you love to look at? What does it make you feel like?

If something makes you feel good, excited, put it in front of you.

With my finger I just click on that Dropbox icon, click open the file folder and I see all these arches and pictures of things I love.

If you can keep yourself inspired there is nothing you cannot do.

What distracts you? Remove yourself from the proximity of the distraction.

I have had people say, "I got so mad, the telephone kept ringing." Well, turn it off. Unplug it. Change your telephone number. I can give you ideas on how to preserve focus.

What unnerves you?

Identify what distracts you. I do not care if it is a person whose ways distract you. Do not let them in your presence. Close the door. Stop it. You have to take some authority in your life. You are authorized to protect your Mind. You are Scripturally authorized. The Holy Spirit will work with you to protect your Mind and your focus.

Fight for it. I do every day. There is a way to handle everything. Find out 3 options and choose one.

Prosperity Is The Fruit of Focus.

Prosperity is the reward of avoiding distractions.

Where are you unlearned? Where are you undeveloped?

One of my people asked me this week, "What do you think my biggest problem is?"

I shared with her, "Because you are experienced you talk condescending to younger people. Because you have the heart of a mother you try to make all the young ladies around you your child and you talk to them like a child."

I said, "Some of them are smarter than you. They know technology and you can't hardly use your phone."

Know where you are unlearned. Know who is learned. Know who is knowledgeable.

I think occasionally about my older sister, Barbara, and my older brother who is a multimillion-aire. He is a very, very successful man. He is smart in business. I am not. I am smart in covenant with God. He is smart in business. Precious man, integrous, one of the sweetest men you would ever know in your life.

So my sister, Barbara, was the first significant World-Class giver I ever experienced. We would go to her house, loved it because she was so generous. She was generous with her food. She is with Jesus now, but she was the first person I ever knew that was generous. But she would give away everything in her business.

She had a Merle Norman shop in West Lake near Lake Charles, Louisiana. People came in and she would give away everything. She could not seem to succeed in business.

She could not seem to get help in business so one day I said, "Barbara, John and I will take off a day, and we are going to fly down and take a look at your business, and we are going to examine it and see what we can do to help save your business."

She flung back like an older sister would to a baby brother, which I will remember forever: "You do not know anything about business."

Well, I have travelled around the world in jets, and stayed in hotels, and printed millions of books...but I do not know anything about business?

Business is exchanging what you have for what somebody else wants. Giving up something you have for what somebody else wants for an agreed reward. Exchanging what they have for what you want. Not a big mystery here. You have a car. Somebody wants it. You exchange what you have. They want it. They give you money for it. It is business.

Who are you refusing to listen to? Who knows what you need to know?

16. Men Stay Poor Because They Will Not Ask Good Questions.

17. Men Stay Poor Because They Will Not Ask For Knowledge.

18. Men Stay Poor Because They Will Not

Ask For Opportunity.

19. Men Stay Poor Because of A Flawed Mentorship.

The whole earth runs by financial rewards.

Some people are bigger problems than the problems they solve.

20. Some Men Stay Poor Because They Make No Effort To Preserve Favor. At some point in your life somebody *liked* you. That is why you are still alive. At some point in your life somebody *protected* you. Somebody spoke well of you. Somebody opened a door of opportunity for you to show your difference. *Everywhere there is a problem there is a Financial Future, and God leaves nobody unrewarded.*

"Father, we could spend 12 hours on this topic and never exhaust it. Thank You for my family and those that are willing to listen to me. Everything You do for me, do for them.

"I ask You boldly Today for new Partners and I am thankful for everyone who holds up my hand as I travel around the world. Thank You, Holy Spirit.

"Father, I ask You to make us teachable. Help us to embrace correction, never to withdraw from correction but embrace it. See its value. Help us to pursue correction, help us to ask for it, request it and be unafraid.

"Lord, I remember the stupid areas of my life where I wanted everybody to correct me a certain way, and I finally realized correction will not come in a certain way. I have to make the adaptation to receive correction.

"The world is not tiptoeing trying to tell us what we are doing wrong. It is a treasure to be corrected. It is pure, sheer gold if somebody exposes what we are doing wrong...it is gold. Our pride will wreck our Prosperity.

"Father, help us not to get picky about who trains us...who teaches us. Help us to find the oil wherever we are. We drill where we are. Under our own soil is our own well of oil! Under our present soil is a Divine well of oil. Praise God. Amen."

I want you to succeed. I am assigned to dreamers.

I do not think any goal that excites you is ludicrous...that God has excited you in His Presence.

Robert Schuller was really a man of great inspiration. It was so sad how some things happened there at Crystal Cathedral out in Garden Grove, California. He really had a desire to teach people so much that he started renting it...people would come up to an outdoor theatre and they could listen to him speak.

He had a marvelous dream and he was really one of the outstanding speakers on positive speaking which is really faith...speaking on what God's promises are.

He used a language that a lot of Christians use so some people did not grasp its importance. But he really had a phenomenal goal of having a glass cathedral with glass windows everywhere. It was beautiful. I used to read a lot of his material years ago.

I am so thankful that God raised up men like him and Norman Vincent Peel and other men. All they were doing was helping God's family see the good in God's world.

Magnify the good around you.

Magnify the good in God's world.

Magnify it so much that it dominates your Mind.

❧ 10 ❧

MILLIONAIRE 300

➤◦◄

"Father, thank You for Psalm 84:11, 'No good thing will You withhold from them that walk uprightly.'

"Thank You, for Psalm 112 that says if we love Your laws, if we Honor Your statutes and commandments, wealth and riches will be in our house.

"Thank You for Deuteronomy 28 that says: If we obey Your commandments that our enemies will be dispersed 7 ways and You will bless us in our coming in and our going out.

"Thank You, Father, for every promise You have made to us.

"Thank You for being a Financial God. You are our Financial God. You are not a dictator. You are not a slave driver. You are not a harsh taskmaster.

You are our Financial God Who is willing and gloriously accessible to discuss how to multiply.

"It is Your will that we prosper and be in health even as our soul prospers as stated in 3 John 2.

"We find You a *caring* God. We find You a *trustworthy* God. We find You to be a *supernatural* God.

"Thank You, Father. Thank You for *teaching* us, *mentoring* us and *protecting* us.

"Thank You for putting inside of us the passion to

multiply, the obsession to increase, and the confidence that we can break the chains of poverty. In the Name of Jesus we pray. Amen. Thank You, Father."

In this chapter I cover *Why Men Stay Poor* and also, *What It Takes To Become A Millionaire.* It doesn't take brains. That is a wonderful glorious relief, isn't it?

I do not have to be a genius.

I do not have to walk in "luck."

I noticed that all the billionaires like to say, "It was just a lot of luck."

Almost no billionaire wants to help other people become wealthy. That is sad.

I have a lot on my heart today.

I had an interesting experience again with a bank yesterday. I had done business with them for years.

I cashed in one of my investments so they direct deposited the funds into the account I designated. Then the bank that received the deposit "restricted" my account.

The deposit was a good bit of money. A lot of people will not make that much in 20 years.

I started saving many years ago, but I decided I did not trust this company anymore.

I do not think there is another human who will have integrity toward my bank account or my money as much as I would. I believe I will be more honest, caring and attentive to my money than any other human I have met will be about my money.

I have not met a single human on the earth who would be more attentive to my money than I would. Neither would I probably be more attentive toward theirs, so that is no big thing.

Your money needs to be in your hands. Your money should never be in other people's hands, unless there is an emergency and that is the only way you can pay a bill.

It took forever for me to get back the money that I had invested. They had been holding my money for 10 years and would not let go of it. I had to fight. I thank God for a lawyer who will fight for me.

By the way, do not ever pay a lawyer any money unless they will fight for you.

Don't hire a lawyer that will not fight for you. That is the whole purpose. They are supposed to be a warrior when you cannot be present. A warrior when you do not know what to do.

I had saved $500,000.00. I had been saving that money, month after month, year after year. I was saving that money for my retirement. That is my money. I have been putting it to the side so that when I get old I will be able to mentor young preachers. I do not want to travel around the world, but be able to focus on writing books.

I got into business deals with all of these companies and I realized, "These are a bunch of unsaved, ungodly people who are about as tricky as you can get."

So I called my attorney and said, "I do not trust any of these companies. If they prove me wrong, that will be glorious." I hope they do prove me wrong, but none of them are racing around to prove integrity.

None of them are obsessed with proving their trustworthiness, but they are obsessed with money.

I understand how the love of money, the obsession

for money, is the root of all evil. I realized for the first time what the Bible was referring to. It meant the obsession for other people's money is the root of all evil. The obsession to survive is not the root of all evil.

Finally, the company released it and sent it to the bank account that I had set aside...$100,000.00 is a lot of money. So, I did not trust this company.

If you have found a company that is diligent, integrous and anxious to get your money to you, wonderful.

At the time I am writing this, I am celebrating receiving one of the greatest Seeds ever planted in my life. It made me shout and dance between the banks.

It took me a good while to get the money sent to my bank account. Before the check of $500,000.00 arrived at the bank, they would not give me the money that was already in my bank account. They said, "Your bank account has been restricted."

They never notified me that they restricted my account. I could not get any money out of my own bank account.

They said, "There has been unusual activity." Whatever that means. Would they tell me what it means? No! Have they ever told me what it means? No! Have I gone to their bank? Yes, about 5 times.

How would you like to have your bank account frozen? They have never notified me. They have my cell number. They have my church number. They have my email address. They have never have notified me.

They just stopped my money flow. I could not do anything. They messed up the PayTrust account I use to pay my bills through. PayTrust can't pay my bills because the bank will not allow them access to my money.

By the time I walked in there $500,000.00 had landed in my bank account.

My attorney involved the Federal Government and suddenly the bank realized there was a possibility for them to be examined because of this activity. They suddenly decided they were going to give my money to me. This was quite an experience.

I went to the bank where I had done business for over 14 years and they pushed five $100,000.00 cashier's checks across the counter. So I had in my hand four $100,000.00 cashier's checks and one for $107,000.00.

I pushed back a $100,000.00 check to them and asked, "Would you cash this now?"

"No, Sir! We do not have enough to cash this check."

I said, "You have my money."

"No, we do not have enough money to cash your check."

They gave me a cashier's check for $507,000.00. Then I asked them to cash that and they said they could not.

Then I asked them to break it up into $100,000.00 segments. They did. Then I handed $100,000.00 back to them and asked, "Would you please cash this?"

"No, we do not have enough."

I said, "Then could you at least break up this $100,000.00 cashier's check into 5 smaller checks of $20,000.00 each.

"Yes, we will do that." So they did that.

Then I pushed the $20,000.00 check back across and asked, "Now, would you cash one of my $20,000 checks?"

"No. We do not have enough money."

I went from bank to bank and none of them could cash it.

Then I got one bank to break a $20,000.00 cashier's check broken up into four $5,000.00 checks.

Are you ready for this?

I went to bank after bank because I do business with 7 banks. None of them could cash a $5,000.00 check.

This is all my money. This is paper they have given me in replacement for my money.

Yesterday I went back to another bank.

"Would you cash this $20,000.00 check?"

"No! We cannot do it."

Then I asked, "Would you turn it into 4 cashier's checks so I can find some bank somewhere that will cash a check for $5,000.00?"

They would not even turn their own cashier's check into four $5,000.00 cashier's checks.

I am holding in my hand the checks that they have written me. They have been printed out to me in my name and they refused to cash their own cashier's checks.

I have done business with this bank for years and they do not have one shred of Honor to even turn their own cashier check into my money. *That is scary.*

I am sitting here with cashier's checks that none of them will cash for me. These are not my checks I have written. The bank that wrote them to me will not cash them.

I had one bank account left open with that bank. They refused to let me deposit their own cashier's checks back in my account.

I do not know if there is a difference in all the banks. There are certainly friendly people in some banks.

This is a dangerous season in American History. I have never in my life seen anything like this.

I am 68. I did not enter the world last week. I have never seen anything like this. I never knew that places would not even cash a cashier's check.

I said, "This is from the bank right across the street."

"We have to call them and verify it."

They may change their Mind after they verify. Banks do not even trust banks. It is like the bank robbers that do not trust each other because they saw the other criminal rob the bank. They rob the bank together so they do not trust each other.

Get attentive to money. I am begging my family be attentive to money.

I am not saying one bank is better than another one. I do not know that they are. I actually do not believe that they are. One bank told me yesterday, "That was a managerial decision."

They have themselves covered so cleverly. I actually suspect that there is a phone number that nobody ever answers, and they use that phone number in front of a customer when they call to get approval. I actually suspect that about 9.5 on a scale of 10.

All I know is that I am shocked that somebody

handling my money acts like I am the culprit. I am the bandit. They are the one with my money. I do not have their money. I do not even have a bank loan. They have my money.

I am very, very attentive to money. If they will do this to Mike Murdock, they will do this to you. They have been doing this, and shafting people for 200 years. Be very careful.

I dare you to go try to get some of your money out. I dare you Today. See if you can get them to give you over $10,000.00 of your own money.

What if you were really in a jam?

If I have some cash I do not have to have that money.

One of them asked, "Why do you want your money?"

"The same reason you want it. I need it."

"What are you going to do with it?" She asked me.

I said, "It is none of your business."

Several asked me what I needed it for. Isn't that stupid? Think of somebody that stupid holding onto your money in a legal trap.

If you think I am just ranting, fine. But, if you believe that this is a Watchman On The Wall, trying to warn you, stay with me.

There are a lot of different things you can do. Get creative with it. I would not tie it all up in real estate because it doesn't mean you can sell it very easily.

Get some gold. It is not a great time for it, but it's better than me spending an entire day of 6 hours going from bank to bank trying to get them to give me my money back.

It would be good if you at least get some gold coins, or something gold. In almost every major city, if you go to Chinatown, you will find someone there who will give you cash for your gold.

1.   Men Stay Poor Because They Do Not Hate Being Poor.

You Can Only Conquer Something You Hate.

Anger Is The Seed For Discovery.

Anger Is The Seed For Recognition.

Anger Is The Seed For Energy.

When you get mad, you get energized.

Anger Is The Seed For New Ideas.

Use your anger in a *productive* way. Do not say: "I am mad. I am really, really mad and I am not going to sit here and act like I am not. Praise God. Hallelujah. Jesus died for me and that is all that matters."

No, that is not all that matters. We have work to do for God. We have an Assignment.

I do not trust anybody that never gets mad. I do not trust you. I sure would not trust your love.

Intensity is part of life. Even God gets mad.

Very sensitive; do not do business with just one bank. *Do not keep all your money in the bank.* Find some options. There are ways to do it. You will get creative.

Find different ways to save money. There are various ways to do it, but the last thing you want is somebody holding onto your money that does not even believe the money belongs to you. That is what I ran into at the banks. They did not believe I had a right to it.

"We have seen something we do not like."

What? What? What is it?

"We will not discuss it. We have just seen some unusual activity."

I think that was the phrase, "unusual activity."

You could have $500,000.00 in their bank and they can say there is been unusual activity and you cannot get a $1.00 bill.

Grasp that folks.

I put $112.00 in my favorite bank. I have an account with $112,000.00 in it.

If you have become a *112 Covenant* Partner, you are going to see the most spectacular year you have ever had in your life.

I had a brother tell me that since they have been planting a $112.00 Seed, Favor unlike anything they have ever seen has begun to come to them.

In fact, one of the men at the church told me the man they are negotiating with came back after they had talked to him and is giving them things all over his house as Favor.

They said, "We have never seen anything like it." He is giving them pieces of furniture. He is giving them all kinds of stuff. They are receiving more Favor than they have ever known in their life.

The 112 Covenant is based on Psalm 112.

If you know the irreplaceable value of somebody's Favor, you ought to invest in *The 112 Covenant* every month.

I do it every week.

One time I did it every day.

Every Sunday morning an auto draft comes to my bank account.

You cannot believe what happens.

2.   Men Stay Poor Because They Do Not Believe They Have Something Worth Millions.

3.   Men Stay Poor Because They Do Not Inventory What God Has Placed Inside of Them.

4.   Men Stay Poor Because They Will Not Pursue With Passion The Advice of Others.

Questions expose truth.

Have you received any paycheck from your job where you kept the Lord's Tithe?

Have you received any birthday present or birthday gift where you kept the Lord's Tithe?

Have you received any bonus from your boss and you kept the Lord's Tithe?

How many books have you read in the last 7 days?

How many books on money have you read? What did you learn? What changes did you make?

Is there a single person that you made a covenant with in purchasing? I was talking to a friend last night about a time share. You made the covenant.

Is there a store you have not paid what you said you would pay them?

Where in your life have you refused to pay what you owe?

Is there anything in your house that you borrowed from someone and never paid back?

Do you owe your mother, father, brother, or sister? Do you owe anybody any money? What has been the regularity of your payback?

Have you bought a car, a television, or any clothes while leaving other people unpaid back for what you told them you would pay them?

Where have you met for financial counsel and what did you pay them? When somebody gave you financial advice, did you follow it?

What can you sell that you own in order to repay somebody you owe?

Do you have two cars? Do you have a car and a truck? Do you have an extra TV? Do you have 3 television sets in your house and you could sell two?

Get things right with God and get things right with people.

Every Wednesday night, we do a Dave Ramsey course at The Wisdom Center. He is the best of the best in America on finances...*how to get out of debt.* If you are not coming, you could watch it online. Every third Wednesday night, you can see it online. It is free.

If you are not a part of it, do not even lie to anybody saying, "I want to learn more about money." You are a liar.

You do not have to come. You do not have to watch it, but do not tell anybody that you are concerned about your finances, because you are not. You are a liar.

Do you know anybody who is doing pretty well financially and has a pretty good understanding of money? What are the last 3 questions you have asked them about money? Did you follow their advice?

I do not have a single person that meets the criteria of a Financial Protégé in my life.

I am not saying you are not a Financial Protégé; you are just not my protégé. I do not have one. I do not have one that meets the criteria of being a true Financial Protégé of financial learning.

Sometimes I feel like Jeremiah. I am doing all this

teaching and it is in vain. I am crazy for doing it. There is so much more I would like to teach besides this.

Last night I told one of my pastors, "I would not concentrate on running across the building cutting off electricity to save $10.00 on my light bill."

I would become skilled in making $100.00.

Our ministry needs a driver.

Our ministry needs a correspondence secretary that loves people enough to answer.

I have a backup of letters I need to write people. I have backed up personal mail right this second that I would pay somebody to help me type out my letters.

I am not interested in hiring somebody who is just willing to work. I need somebody who is willing to become skilled, trained and taught.

I have a wonderful job position for an App Developer. I will pay you good money to develop Apps I want developed.

I have a job position for someone who will find an App Developer and get a job done instead of talking about it every day.

To become a millionaire you have to be willing to *solve* problems. *You start with what you can.*

To be my personal driver, you will need to use a paper map, not just GPS. You need to use a paper map because GPS people get lost 7 out of 10 times and I have got proof. To be my driver, you need to be able to follow my instructions easily. I will pay for the Atlas. You just have to look at the map.

I would give anything to have a driver who will buy a map and look at it. I have never been able to find a single human who will look at a paper map and show me where we are. I would consider a female chauffeur. The problem is when you are single you do not need to be running around alone with a woman; you need some men around. Think about that!

A young preacher worked for me for a long time and he drove me everywhere. I got so mad because he refused to buy a map. The last time I let him drive for me, we blundered around for an hour looking for a place. Finally, I got so frustrated I told him to pull over at a convenience store, go inside and buy a map.

He came back out and I asked to see the map. He hand written the directions on a piece of paper and gave it to me. He still had not bought a map! I got so mad at him. He quit after 30 days.

I went ahead and gave him $10,000.00 to start his church. He wanted to start a church. He is a good young man; he just will not follow instructions. He is likable.

I do not think anybody is good that does not follow instructions. He is likeable. He is lovable. A lot of folks are lovable.

I do not know if you are good if you will not follow my instructions. I do not know how any human is good that will not follow the instructions of the man who is paying him. I cannot call you good to take my paycheck, but will not do what I ask.

Anyway, I sense that there may be somebody that will buy a map and even look at it.

What does it take to be a millionaire?

Embrace opportunities to solve problems.

Be trustworthy; do what you say; do not slick and slither and slide.

Honor the people in your life that give you counsel.

Honor a man that will pay you to follow an instruction.

What does it take to become a millionaire?

Believe that money is better than poverty. That is all. Just believe that money is better than poverty.

Prosperity is Scriptural.

Prosperity is a God thing.

What does it take to be a millionaire?

Develop a reputation for credibility, for Prosperity.

Do what you are asked. Do what you are told. Follow the instructions.

Find a job that you love. If you do not like your job, quit. Find a job that makes you want to wake up early every day. Believe in the person you are working for. Believe that problem solving will be Divinely rewarded if not humanly rewarded.

What does it take to become a millionaire? *Admire one. Honor one. Listen to one. Study their decisions.* Study the decisions of somebody who is a millionaire. Listen to them. Stay close.

Become the major problem-solver in a successful person's life.

What does it take to become a millionaire?

Make it your focus.

Make God your Partner.

Never lie. Never lie. Never lie. Never lie.

Resist the spirit of laziness.

Resist the spirit of lying.

Get your house in order.

Get your finances in order.

Do not spend any money you do not have to.

Learn how to spend money in a way that inspires you.

Read my book, 31 Reasons People Do Not Receive Their Financial Harvest. It will change your world.

"Father, I told You at the beginning of my ministry that I would always teach what I felt like was important to the family and I am doing it today.

"Some know its value. Some do not.

"I ask You to break the spirit of poverty in our life. Give us a hatred for lack. Give us a hatred for laziness. Show us the Law of Honor on how to make good things happen for people.

"Father, I ask You to bring people to my ministry who will Honor my instructions, in Jesus' Name. Amen."

Family, if possible, and if you are willing, I would enter *The 112 Covenant.* This is a Seed of $112.00 a month. Not one penny will go into my pocket. You can sow it into the ministry. You can put it on auto draft once a month.

I want to see you do it for 12 months and document and journal the streams of Favor.

If Somebody Likes You, You Will Never Be Broke A Day In Your Life.

If you solve problems somebody will show you Favor.

Everywhere There Is Favor There Is Money.

God schedules surprises of ecstasy for people who really believe His Word.

Do not go another day without Divine Partnership. God can give you one idea that will unlock $20,000.00. Just one idea.

In every environment, somebody is authorized to change the rules for you.

11

KNOW THE TRUE SOURCE OF INCREASE

"Father, thank You for a glorious day in Your presence. Thank You from my heart for all those who experienced a public confession that You are their God. You are their Lord. Thank You for our church family who know the value, the benefits, the improvements, the changes that are birthed in Your Presence. Especially in Your manifested Presence.

"Thank You, Lord, You have touched my heart with this subject *Why Men Stay Poor.* Enable me to ignite in the family of God a passion to do business with You, to enter into a covenant where our hidden gifts are ignited, activated, processed, marketed.

"You gave...levels of talents. Some one, some two, some 5, some 10. We know the value of Divine genius unlocked in us. I thank You for this message that burns in my heart in Jesus' Name."

I have a real experience with the Lord...His blessings. There are so many parts of God...like planets, Neptune, Pluto, Mars, Jupiter. There are so many different experiences you can have with God.

His creativity that reveals His needs. The same God who created the dinosaur created the squirrel, the skunk, the roach, the deer, the bear, the lion. Our God is way beyond the limitation of our experience.

There is so much to God. No man can begin to know *all* of God. But there is a part of God that is real vital to an effective life and it is the financial philosophy.

Men Stay Poor Because They Do Not Know The Heart of God. They do not understand the pleasure and the ecstasy God gets in giving.

I got mad at a girlfriend one time. I could not imagine, I did not know why I was so mad. What it was is, every time I wanted to give her something she did something to slap it down. I could not give to her what I wanted to give to her.

God giving to us brings Him superb pleasure...*if you are not a giver you do not understand this.* Believe me, you do not understand this. If you are a person who loves to bless people, you love to find a reason to bless them. You have to qualify to receive from God, and that is why we sing the song, *Qualify Me, Qualify Me.*

I do not know of anybody who *struggles* as much as God struggles to reveal who He is. Psalm 84:11 says, "No good thing will He withhold from those that walk uprightly." If ye being evil know how to give good gifts to your children, how much more your Heavenly Father love to give to those...God is love. (Read Matthew 7:11.) Think about that. God is love. "For God so loved that He gave." (See John 3:16.) Giving is equal to your love. *Giving reveals your love.*

Now imagine the God of the Universe...Jesus said it, "God is love." That is who He is, He loves. *He has a passion to bless us.* So extensive He has given you a list of things that He wants to give to you. Look at Leviticus 26; Deuteronomy 28.

Until you understand God, understand the heart of God, you can do things that disqualify you from receiving from Him and there are many people that do not even know this part of God.

There is a pastor here in Dallas that speaks Greek and Hebrew but publicly announced healing as a farce and a sham and that Benny Hinn and all those that believed in healing were false. One preacher even made the statement that people were paid to give testimonies. He said Jesus did not heal today.

This man speaks Greek and Hebrew and he des not believe in the healing part of Jesus. But if you have not experienced that part of God, and you have been trained in error...remember that Mentorship decides the speed to your destination.

Who are you willing to learn from? You learn at the pace...the speed of your questions. That is powerful to me. That is so, so powerful in my opinion.

Jesus wanted us to know the nature of God. I want people to know Him so badly that I will tell illustrations that make me look like an idiot sometimes, because I want them to know the variation of my life. I feel like it takes the stress off of a relationship. I want them to know me. I am very direct, very frank, very exact in what I like and what I do not like and I am very outspoken.

Silence is the weapon for secrets. Silence is very different from discretion. I am very happy, very thrilled that the God I know about is so conversational. I really like meaningful conversation, purposeful conversation.

Jesus said, "I have come so you will know what the Father is like. And when you have seen Me you have seen the Father." Isn't that wonderful?

1 *M*oney...Is Unimportant To You..?
...That Explains Its Absence.

2 *I*s Your Guilt Over Money About...
...Having Too Much of It or...
...Not Having Enough?

3 *M*oney Is What You Receive...When You
Help Someone Else Achieve Their Goal.

4 *Y*our Money *Movement*...Shows Your
Money *Weaknesses*.

5 *M*en Stay Poor Because They Don't
Know The Character of God.

6 *A* Problem...Is The Golden Door
To An Opportunity.
...Relationship.
...$$ Reward.
...Change.
...Significance.

7 *E*verywhere You Sow Honor...
You Will Reap Favor.
Everywhere You Find Favor...
You Will Find $.

8 *F*avor...Is Worth Protecting.
Few-Know-It.

9 **M**oney Grows...
Wherever You Planted Honor.
Few-Get-It.

10 **M**ONEY IS...Anywhere God
Wanted You To Be.

11 **M**oney Is Not The Destination;
It Is The BRIDGE To Your Destination.
(A Tool...Weapon...Key...)

12 **Y**our Success...Is Not God's *Decision*.
Your Success...Is God's *Desire*.

13 **S**uccess Is The Reward...
For Asking Enough Questions.

Money Is The Reward...
For Solving Problems.

14 **T**hose Critical of Money...
Disqualify Themselves For It.

15 **M**oney Is Not A Miracle.
Money Is Not A Mystery.
Money Is...Simply The Reward System For
Solving Problems.

16 **M**ONEY IS...Anywhere God
Wanted You To Be.

*M*oney Is...

The Seed For New Experiences.

-Mike Murdock

*M*oney:

Something You Need

To Create What You Love.

-*Mike Murdock*

Money Is...

A Pain-Remover.
Marvelously So.

-Mike Murdock

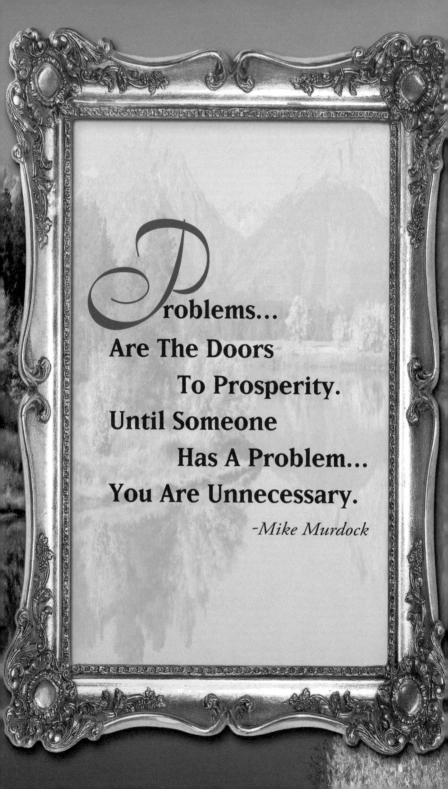

Problems...
Are The Doors
        To Prosperity.
Until Someone
        Has A Problem...
You Are Unnecessary.

-*Mike Murdock*

Holy Spirit, Move Again

Words and Music by Mike Murdock

Sweet Holy Spirit, Do Your work in me;

Sweet Holy Spirit, I'm ready to receive;

Sweet Holy Spirit, I will never grieve Your name

All I ask of You Holy Spirit move again.

~Joel 2:28-29~

And it shall come to pass afterward, that I will pour out My spirit upon all flesh; and your sons and your daughters shall prophesy, your old men shall dream dreams, your young men shall see visions:

And also upon the servants and upon the handmaids in those days will I pour out My spirit.

~Acts 2:1-4~

And when the day of Pentecost was fully come, they were all with one accord in one place.

And suddenly there came a sound from heaven as of a rushing mighty wind, and it filled all the house where they were sitting.

And there appeared unto them cloven tongues like as of fire, and it sat upon each of them.

And they were all filled with the Holy Ghost, and began to speak with other tongues, as the Spirit gave them utterance.

Fill This Place With Your Presence

Words and Music by Mike Murdock

Fill this place with Your Presence.

Fill this place with Your Presence.

Fill this place with Your Presence

until nothing that grieves You remains.

Fill this place with Your Glory.

Fill this place with Your Glory.

Fill this place with Your Glory

until nothing that grieves You remains.

Fill this place with Your Wisdom.

Fill this place with Your Wisdom.

Fill this place with Your Wisdom

until nothing that grieves You remains.

I Let Go
(of Anything That Stops Me)

Words and Music by Mike Murdock

I let go of anything that stops me.

I let go of anything that slows me down.

I let go of anything that breaks my focus on You.

Holy Spirit, Holy Spirit, I let go.

~Hebrews 12:1~

Wherefore seeing we also are compassed about with so great a cloud of witnesses, let us lay aside every weight, and the sin which doth so easily beset us, and let us run with patience the race that is set before us.

~Matthew 18:8-9~

Wherefore if thy hand or thy foot offend thee, cut them off, and cast them from thee: it is better for thee to enter into life halt or maimed, rather than having two hands or two feet to be cast into everlasting fire.

And if thine eye offend thee, pluck it out, and cast it from thee: it is better for thee to enter into life with one eye, rather than having two eyes to be cast into hell fire.

I Live For The Anointing

Words and Music by Mike Murdock

I live for the anointing;
It's the presence of the Holy One.
I live for the anointing,
For from it victories are won;
Ev'ry demon has to bow down
in the presence of the Son,
I live for the anointing,
I live for the anointing,
I live for the anointing;
It's the presence of the Holy One.

~Isaiah 10:27~

And it shall come to pass in that day, that His burden shall be taken away from off thy shoulder, and His yoke from off thy neck, and the yoke shall be destroyed because of the anointing.

~1 John 2:27~

But the anointing which ye have received of Him abideth in you, and ye need not that any man teach you: but as the same anointing teacheth you of all things, and is truth, and is no lie, and even as it hath taught you, ye shall abide in Him.

Harvest REPORTS

One of Many Miracles..! I felt as if I was having a heart attack in my sleep; and I had my husband take me to the emergency room. After many EKG's with irregular readings and further testing on my arteries, the baffled specialist said that my arteries and heart were perfect... the prettiest he had ever seen! This is one of the many miracles I've had since planting the $58 Seed..!

M. C., Newburgh (UK)

God Honored My Seed..! I sowed a $58 Seed for my daughter to get a job in nursing and for her not to lose her home. God honored my Seed. She got 3 different offers for nursing jobs; and she was able to keep her home! We serve a mighty God..!

A. D., New York, NY

Healing..! Early in 2010, I was diagnosed with a lump in my breast. The doctor suggested therapy, but, I waited on God for the right decision. In November, I mailed a $58 Seed. A week later, I had my last mammogram and no lump could be found..!

A. C., Rowland Heights, CA

Breakthrough Court Settlement..! After sending a $58 Seed to you, I got miracle money sent to me in the mail and a breakthrough in a court settlement! Praise God..!

D. T., Columbus, OH

Harvest REPORTS

Received Extra Money..! I wanted to sow a Seed into your ministry, but I needed extra funds. When my storage bill came due, it was discounted, enabling me to give a $58 Seed! After sowing it, I unexpectedly received $159..!

K. S., Los Altos Hills, CA

Miracle Healing..! My daughter has been estranged from me for the last 15 years. She was diagnosed with uterine cancer on September 25. And she developed another condition in her abdomen called septicemia that has a history of only 5% survival rate. I sowed $58 and later gave 1 week's salary to your ministry. Within 4 days, God healed her completely! All her test results showed negative on December 10!! Her ex-mother-in-law is paying ALL her bills!!! And, God has restored her relationship with me! What an awesome God..!!!

D. E., Haltom City, TX

$58 Seed For Every Family Member..! I heard you say that you sowed a $58 Seed for every member of your family. So I did it, too. Since then, my father collected on a job he did, that he had never been paid for. My mother got back child support and received her tax returns. And my brother received help from my father to pay his credit card bill. Praise God..!

S. H., Los Angeles, CA

Healed of Depression..! I began sowing $58 Seeds to your ministry…specifically for the purpose of being healed from depression. I can now testify that I have been healed from 24 years of depression.

Lee B., Sebring, FL

DECISION

Will You Accept Jesus As Your Personal Savior Today?

The Bible says, "That if thou shalt confess with thy mouth the Lord Jesus, and shalt believe in thine heart that God hath raised Him from the dead, thou shalt be saved," (Romans 10:9).

Pray this prayer from your heart today!

"Dear Jesus, I believe that You died for me and rose again on the third day. I confess I am a sinner...I need Your love and forgiveness...Come into my heart. Forgive my sins. I receive Your eternal life. Confirm Your love by giving me peace, joy and supernatural love for others. Amen."

DR. MIKE MURDOCK

is in tremendous demand as one of the most dynamic speakers in America today.

More than 23,000 audiences in over 100 countries have attended his Schools of Wisdom and conferences. Hundreds of invitations come to him from churches, colleges and business corporations. He is a noted author of over 300 books, including the best sellers, *The Leadership Secrets of Jesus* and *Secrets of the Richest Man Who Ever Lived*. Thousands view his weekly television program, *Wisdom Keys with Mike Murdock*. Many attend his Schools of Wisdom that he hosts in many cities of America.

☐ Yes, Mike, I made a decision to accept Christ as my personal Savior today. Please send me my free gift of your book, *31 Keys to a New Beginning* to help me with my new life in Christ.

NAME   BIRTHDAY

ADDRESS

CITY   STATE   ZIP

PHONE   EMAIL   DFC

Mail to: **The Wisdom Center** · 4051 Denton Hwy. · Ft. Worth, TX 76117
1-817-759-BOOK · 1-817-759-2665 · 1-817-759-0300
You Will Love Our Website..! MikeMurdockBooks.com

14 Harvests Are Waiting For You..!

Dear Friend,

God has connected us!

I have asked The Holy Spirit for 3000 Special Partners who will plant a monthly Seed of $58.00 to help me bring the gospel around the world. (58 represents 58 kinds of blessings in the Bible.)

Will you become my monthly Faith Partner in The Wisdom Key 3000? Your monthly Seed of $58.00 is so powerful in helping heal broken lives. When you sow into the work of God, 4 Miracle Harvests are guaranteed in Scripture, Isaiah 58...

▸ Uncommon <u>Health</u> (Isaiah 58)
▸ Uncommon <u>Wisdom</u> For <u>Decision-Making</u> (Isaiah 58)
▸ Uncommon <u>Financial Favor</u> (Isaiah 58)
▸ Uncommon <u>Family Restoration</u> (Isaiah 58)

I would love to hear from you. Email me today at
DrMurdock@TheWisdomCenter.tv..!

Your Faith Partner,

Mike Murdock

P.S. Will You Become My Ministry Partner In The Work of God?

PP-03

☐ **Please Rush My Mentorship 10 Pak..! Yes, Mike, I Want To Join The Wisdom Key 3000.**

☐ **Enclosed Is My First Monthly Seed-Faith Promise of:** ☐ **$58** ☐ **Other $_____.**

☐ CHECK   ☐ MONEY ORDER   ☐ AMEX   ☐ DISCOVER   ☐ MASTERCARD   ☐ VISA

Credit Card # _____ Exp. _____/_____

Signature _____

Name _____ Birth Date _____/_____

Address _____

City _____ State _____ Zip _____

Phone _____ E-Mail _____

THE WISDOM CENTER
4051 Denton Highway • Fort Worth, TX 76117

Office: 1-817-759-0300
Order: 1-817-759-BOOK (2665)

You Will Love Our Website..!
MikeMurdockBooks.com

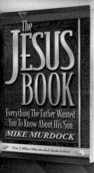

Crisis 7 BOOK PAK!

❶ The Survival Bible (Book/B-29/248pg/$12)

❷ Wisdom For Crisis Times (Book/B-40/112pg/$9)

❸ Seeds of Wisdom on Motivating Yourself (Book/B-171/32pg/$5)

❹ Seeds of Wisdom on Overcoming (Book/B-17/32pg/$5)

❺ Seeds of Wisdom on Warfare (Book/B-19/32pg/$5)

❻ Battle Techniques For War Weary Saints (Book/B-07/32pg/$5)

❼ Seeds of Wisdom on Adversity (Book/B-21/32pg/$5)

*Each Wisdom Book may be purchased separately if so desired.

The Wisdom Center
Crisis 7 Book Pak!
Only $**30** $45 Value
WBL-25
Wisdom Is The Principal Thing

Add 20% For S/H

Quantity Prices Available Upon Request

Career 7

Book Pak For Business People!

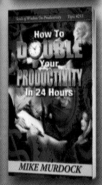

DR. MIKE MURDOCK

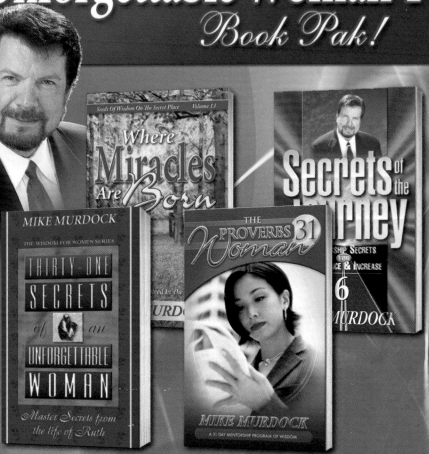

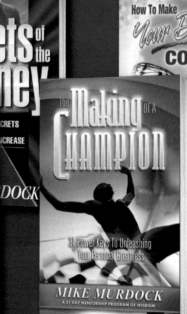

Increase 4 *Book Pak!*

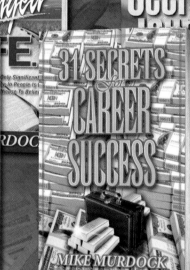

❶ The Book That Changed My Life... (Book/B-117/32pg/$7)

❷ Secrets of The Journey, Vol. 2 (Book/B-93/32pg/$5)

❸ 7 Keys to 1000 Times More
(Book/B-104/128pg/$10)

❹ 31 Secrets for Career Success
(Book/B-44/112pg/$12)

Wisdom Book may be purchased separately if so desired.

THE WISDOM CENTER
4051 Denton Highway · Fort Worth, TX 76117

1-817-759-BOOK
1-817-759-2665
1-817-759-0300

You Will Love Our Website..!
MIKEMURDOCKBOOKS.COM

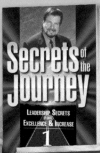
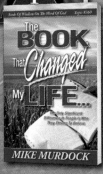

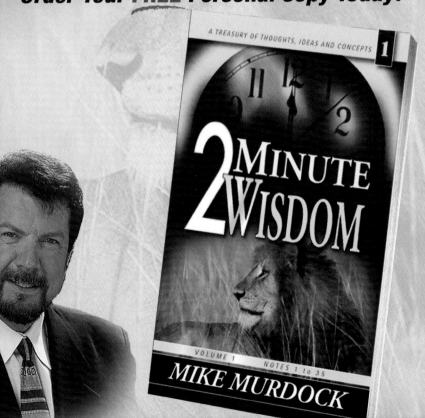

THE WISDOM BIBLE

Partnership Edition

Over 120 Wisdom Study Guides Included Such As:

▸ *10 Qualities of Uncommon Achievers*
▸ *18 Facts You Should Know About The Anointing*
▸ *21 Facts To Help You Identify Those Assigned To You*
▸ *31 Facts You Should Know About Your Assignment*
▸ *8 Keys That Unlock Victory In Every Attack*
▸ *22 Defense Techniques To Remember During Seasons of Personal Attack*
▸ *20 Wisdom Keys And Techniques To Remember During An Uncommon Battle*
▸ *11 Benefits You Can Expect From God*
▸ *31 Facts You Should Know About Favor*
▸ *The Covenant of 58 Blessings*
▸ *7 Keys To Receiving Your Miracle*
▸ *16 Facts You Should Remember About Contentious People*
▸ *5 Facts Solomon Taught About Contracts*
▸ *7 Facts You Should Know About Conflict*
▸ *6 Steps That Can Unlock Your Self-Confidence*
▸ *And Much More!*

Your Partnership makes such a difference in The Wisdom Center Outreach Ministries. I wanted to place a Gift in your hand that could last a lifetime for you and your family...**The Wisdom Study Bible.**

40 Years of Personal Notes...this Partnership Edition Bible contains 160 pages of my Personal Study Notes...that could forever change your Bible Study of The Word of God. This **Partnership Edition...**is my personal **Gift of Appreciation** when you sow your Sponsorship Seed of $1,000 for our Television Outreach Ministry. An Uncommon Seed Always Creates An Uncommon Harvest!

Mike

Thank you from my heart for your Seed of Obedience (Luke 6:38).

L

THE WISDOM CENTER
WISDOM CENTER
4051 Denton Highway • Fort Worth, TX 76117

1-817-759-BOOK
1-817-759-2665
1-817-759-0300

— *You Will Love Our Website..!*
MIKEMURDOCKBOOKS.COM

This Gift of Appreciation Will Change Your Bible Study For The Rest of Your Life.

The Wisdom Bible

MY GIFT OF APPRECIATION

Celebrating Your Sponsorship Seed of $1,000 For Our Television Outreach Ministry.

B-235

Wisdom Is The Principal Thing

7 Hidden Ingredients In Every Miracle...

The Hidden Secrets That Cause Miracles To Happen.

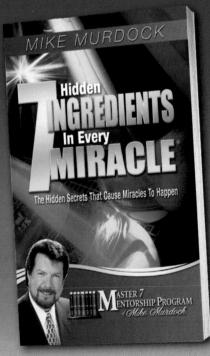

You Will Learn:

▶ *How To Apply The Scriptural Formula In Every Prayer*

▶ *3 Ways To Build Your Faith To Mountain-Moving Level*

▶ *Why Some Miracles Are Delayed Unnecessarily*

▶ *The Hidden Prescription For Silencı Demonic Voices In Your Environme.*

The Wisdom Center

ONLY $7

B-280

Wisdom Is The Principal Thing

N

THE WISDOM CENTER
4051 Denton Highway · Fort Worth, TX 76117

1-817-759-BOOK
1-817-759-2665
1-817-759-0300

You Will Love Our Website..!
MIKEMURDOCKBOOKS.COM

14 Harvests Are Waiting For You..!

Dear Friend,

God has connected us!

I have asked The Holy Spirit for 3000 Special Partners who will plant a monthly Seed of $58.00 to help me bring the gospel around the world. (58 represents 58 kinds of blessings in the Bible.)

Will you become my monthly Faith Partner in The Wisdom Key 3000? Your monthly Seed of $58.00 is so powerful in helping heal broken lives. When you sow into the work of God, 4 Miracle Harvests are guaranteed in Scripture, Isaiah 58...

- ▶ Uncommon <u>Health</u> (Isaiah 58)
- ▶ Uncommon <u>Wisdom</u> For <u>Decision-Making</u> (Isaiah 58)
- ▶ Uncommon <u>Financial Favor</u> (Isaiah 58)
- ▶ Uncommon <u>Family Restoration</u> (Isaiah 58)

Your Faith Partner,

Mike Murdock

P.S. Will You Become My Ministry Partner In The Work of God?

PP-03

☐ *Please Rush My Mentorship 10 Pak..! Yes, Mike, I Want To Join The Wisdom Key 3000.*

☐ *Enclosed Is My First Monthly Seed-Faith Promise of:* ☐ *$58* ☐ *Other $_____.*

☐CHECK ☐MONEY ORDER ☐AMEX ☐DISCOVER ☐MASTERCARD ☐V

Credit Card # _____ Exp. _____/__

Signature _____

Name _____ Birth Date _____/__

Address _____

City _____ State _____ Zip _____

Phone _____ E-Mail _____

 THE WISDOM CENTER
4051 Denton Highway · Fort Worth, TX 76117

1-817-759-BOOK
1-817-759-2665
1-817-759-0300

You Will Love Our Website..!
MikeMurdockBooks.com